May man prevail?

Erich Fromm, a psychoanalyst of world-wide reputation, left his native Germany in 1932 to come to the United States. In addition to his psychiatric work and his teaching activities, he has published several books since his arrival here. In *May Man Prevail?* he offers an analysis of world politics based on his long and exhaustive studies of Karl Marx as well as Sigmund Freud.

May man prevail?

AN INQUIRY INTO THE FACTS
AND FICTIONS OF FOREIGN POLICY

by Erich Fromm

ANCHOR BOOKS

Doubleday & Company, Inc.

GARDEN CITY, NEW YORK

Communist China and Asia by A. Doak Barnett. Published
by Harper & Brothers for the Council on Foreign Relations. Reprinted with permission. *Russian Youth Asks Some
Questions* by Marvin Kalb; The *New York Times* magazine, April 23, 1961; reprinted by permission of the author;
© 1961, by The New York Times Company. *Stalin* by Isaac
Deutscher. Published by Oxford University Press, Inc. Reprinted with permission. *On Thermonuclear War* by Herman Kahn. Published 1960 by Princeton University Press.
Reprinted with permission. *The Future as History* by Rob-
ert L. Heilbroner. *The United States in the World Arena*
by W. W. Rostow. Reprinted by permission of Harper &
Brothers. *The Necessity for Choice* by Henry A. Kissinger.
Published by Harper & Brothers. Published by Chatto &
Windus in 1961. Reprinted with permission. *Russia, the
Atom and the West* by George F. Kennan. Reprinted by
permission of Harper & Brothers and Oxford University
Press. *The Soviet Bloc: Unity and Conflict* by Zbigniew K.
Brzezinski. Copyright 1960 by The President and Fellows
of Harvard College. Reprinted by permission of Harvard
University Press. *The Question of National Defense* by
Oskar Morgenstern. Copyright © 1959 by Oskar Morgen-
stern. Reprinted by permission of Random House, Inc.
Marx's Concept of Man by Erich Fromm; with *Marx's Ec-
onomic and Philosophical Manuscripts* translated by T. B.
Bottomore. Published 1961 by Frederick Ungar Publishing
Co., Inc. Reprinted by permission of T. B. Bottomore and
Frederick Ungar Publishing Co., Inc. *Soviet Foreign Policy,
1917–1941* by George F. Kennan. Copyright 1960 by D.
van Nostrand Co., Inc., Princeton, New Jersey. Reprinted
by permission of the publisher.

Anchor Books edition: 1961

Published simultaneously in a hardbound edition by
Doubleday & Company, Inc.

Acknowledgments

I want to express my gratitude to Roger Hagan who has not only helped me in the gathering of historical material but has made many important critical and constructive suggestions in reference to the whole manuscript. I also owe sincere thanks to Michael Maccoby who has contributed valuable suggestions, especially to the chapter on disarmament; and to Harrop Freeman who took time out of a heavy schedule to read the manuscript thoroughly and to make important suggestions. I also thank David Riesman and Stewart Meacham for reading the manuscript shortly before the final printing and for making significant suggestions and criticisms.   E. F.

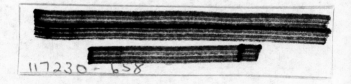

117230 - 658

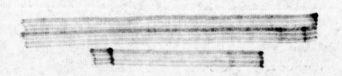

Preface

There is little disagreement among responsible political leaders that the United States and the whole Western world are passing through a dangerous period. Even though opinions vary on the degree of these dangers, there is a widely shared conviction that we have a clear and realistic picture of the situation, that we are meeting it as adequately as we can, and that there is no essentially different course of action we can take. The premises on which this opinion of the world situation is based are largely the following:

Communism, represented by the Soviet Union and China, is a revolutionary-imperialist movement out to conquer the world by force or subversion. Its industrial and military development has made the Communist camp, and particularly the Soviet Union, into a powerful rival, capable of destroying our human and industrial potential to a considerable degree. This bloc can be restrained from executing its wish for world conquest solely by the knowledge that any such attempt would be met with a counterblow that would destroy or cripple its human and economic potential. In this deterrent capacity lies the only hope for peace since Russia will abstain from her attempt at world conquest only because of fear of our deterrent. As long as we have a sufficiently strong deterrent power and military allies around the world, peace is secured.

Within this general concept, opinions vary widely. There are those who consider that while nuclear warfare may kill 60 to 70 million Americans it will not destroy or seriously transform our form of life. There are others who consider the probability of losses of 100 to 150 million casualties as being more realistic. There are those who are in favor of disarmament negotiations from a position of strength, while others look at any kind of disarmament negotiations as a futile exercise in propaganda. There are those who are for limited steps toward arms control, like the cessation of nuclear tests, while there are others who consider any such step a threat to our security. There are those who favor a nuclear strategy of counterforce aimed at the enemy's missile bases, and those who favor a "second strike" stable deterrent, aimed at the population centers, and still others who try to combine both strategies. (Although this combination may deprive both approaches of their alleged advantages.) Views also differ in various sectors of our policy-making groups. Under the Eisenhower administration, the State Department and the President took a somewhat more conciliatory line with regard to the cessation of testing and arms control, while the military and the Atomic Energy Commission have then and now taken a less conciliatory stand. The various armed services differ among themselves in strategic concepts. Each espouses a concept that provides the most room for its own expansion and at the same time makes some compromises with its two competing services.

In spite of these differences, however, most responsible political leaders and the majority of the population seem convinced of the correctness of the basic premises of our policy and appear willing to continue in the direction we have taken. Indeed they are certain that there is no other possible course—in fact, that every other course is more conducive to war than the one we are taking. This position is buttressed by the conviction that our policy is not only the sole hope for physical survival, but that it is also the only one recommended by moral and spiritual considerations. They believe that we and our allies represent freedom and idealism, while the Russians and their allies represent servitude and materialism. The assumption is made that the risk of even war and destruction must be taken because it is better to die than to be slaves.

When executing a policy based on these premises, anyone who knows the dangers involved for us and for the whole world will have a heavy heart, but few doubts. He will be convinced that we are doing the best we can, and that there is no other course of action which can protect us better from war or enslavement.

If, however, the premises on which our policy is based are erroneous then, indeed, we would be taking a course of action that no human being with some sense of responsibility and duty could dare to recommend. Hence, we have the intellectual and moral obligation to question the correctness of these premises again and again. I wish to contribute to this questioning. I shall try to demonstrate the reasons for my conviction that many of the premises on which our policy is based are untrue, that many of our assumptions are fictitious or distorted, and hence that we are running with confused minds into the gravest danger for ourselves and the rest of mankind.

Many a reader may be surprised or shocked by some of my statements and conclusions; all I ask of him is that he keep an open mind, and that he follow my argument with a minimum of emotional bias. After all, most of us share two concerns: we do not want an all-destructive war, and we do want the ideas of human dignity and individualism to be kept alive on this earth. I will try to demonstrate that peace is still possible and that the humanist tradition has, still, a future.

Contents

Contents

May man prevail?

CHAPTER ONE

Some general premises

I) ANTICIPATORY VERSUS CATASTROPHIC CHANGE

Societies have lives of their own; they are based on the existence of certain productive forces, geographical and climatic conditions, techniques of production, ideas and values, and a certain type of human character that develops under these conditions. They are organized in such a way that they tend to continue existing in the particular form to which they have adapted themselves. Usually, men in each society believe that the mode in which they exist is natural and inevitable. They hardly see any other possibilities and, in fact, they tend to believe that a basic change in their own mode of existence would lead to chaos and destruction. They are seriously convinced that their way is right, sanctioned by the gods or by the laws of human nature, and that the only alternative to the continuation of the particular form in which they exist is destruction. This belief is not simply the result of indoctrination; it is rooted in the affective part of man, in his *character structure*, which is molded by all social and cultural arrangements so that man *wants to do what he has to do*, so that his energy is channeled in such a way as to serve the particular function he has to fulfill as a useful member of a given society. It is for this very reason, namely that the patterns of *thought* are rooted in patterns of *feeling*, that patterns of thought are so very persistent and resistant to change.

Yet societies do change. Many factors, like new productive forces, scientific discoveries, political conquests, expansion of population, and so on, make for change. In addition to these objective factors, man's growing awareness of his needs and of himself and, most of all, of his increasing need for freedom and independence, make for constant change in his historical situation, ranging from the cave dweller's existence to the space-traveling man of the near future.

How do these changes occur?

Most of them have occurred in violent and catastrophic ways. Most societies, leaders and led, have been incapable of adapting themselves voluntarily and peacefully to fundamentally new conditions *by anticipating the necessary changes.* They have tended to go on and on with what they sometimes poetically called "accomplishing their mission," trying to continue the basic pattern of their social lives with only small changes and modifications. Even when circumstances that were in complete and flagrant contradiction to their whole structure arose such societies went on blindly trying to continue their modes of living until they could not manage any further. They were then conquered and destroyed by other nations, or they slowly died because of their incapacity to master life any longer in their customary way.

Those most opposed to fundamental change have been the élites, which profited most from the existing order and hence were unwilling to give up their privileges voluntarily. But the material interests of the ruling and privileged groups are not the only reason for the incapacity of many cultures to anticipate necessary changes. Another equally important reason lies in a psychological factor. Leaders and led, having hypostatized and deified their way of life, their thought concepts, and their formulation of values, become rigidly committed to them. Even only slightly different concepts become intensely disturbing and are looked upon as hostile, devilish, crazy attacks on one's own 'normal,' 'sound' thinking.

For the Cromwellians, the Papists were of the Devil; for the Jacobeans, the Girondists; for the Americans, the Communists. Man, in each society, seems to absolutize the way of life and the way of thought produced by his culture and to be willing to die rather than to change, since change, to him, is equated with death. Thus the history of man is a graveyard of great cultures that came to catastrophic ends because of their incapacity for planned, rational, voluntary reaction to challenge.

Yet nonviolent anticipatory change has also occurred in history. The liberation of the working class from the status of objects of ruthless exploitation to that of influential economic partners in Western industrialized society is an example of nonviolent change in the class relations within societies. The willingness of the British Labour Government to grant independence to India before it was forced to do so is an example in the area of international relations. But these anticipatory solutions have been the exceptions rather than the rule in history, so far. Religious peace came to Europe only *after* the Thirty Years' War, to England only after violent and cruel mutual persecution by Papists and anti-Papists alike; in the First and Second World Wars, peace came only after the futile slaughter of millions of men and women on both sides and long after the eventual outcome of the war was already clear. Would not mankind have gained if the enforced decisions had been voluntarily accepted by both sides *before* they were enforced? Would not an anticipatory compromise have averted hideous losses and wholesale brutalization?

Today we are facing again one of the crucial choices in which the difference between violent versus anticipatory solution may spell the difference between destruction and fertile growth of our civilization. Today's world is divided into two blocs confronting each other with suspicion and hate. Both blocs have the capacity to harm each other to a degree the magnitude of which is equalled only by the inexactitude of its measurement. (The estimates of losses the United States can expect vary from one-third to practically the whole of its population being wiped out in a nuclear war—and similar estimates are applicable to the Soviet Union.) The two blocs are fully armed and prepared for war. They distrust each other, and each suspects the other of wanting to conquer and destroy it. The present equilibrium of suspicion and threat based on a destructive potential may yet last for a little while. But in the long run the only alternatives are nuclear war and all its consequences on the one hand, or the ending of the cold war, which implies disarmament and political peace between the two blocs, on the other.

The question is, must the United States (and her Western allies) and the Soviet Union, and Communist China each pursue its present course to the bitter end, or can both sides anticipate certain changes and arrive at a solution that is historically possible and that, at the same time, offers optimal advantages to each bloc.

The question is essentially the same as that which other societies and cultures have been confronted with; namely, whether we *are capable of applying historical understanding to political action.*[1]

And here the subsidiary question arises: what is it that makes a society viable, allowing it to respond to change? There is no simple answer, but clearly the society must above all be able to discriminate its primary values from its secondary values and institutions. This is difficult because secondary systems generate values of their own, which come to appear as essential as the human and social needs which brought them into being. As people's lives become intertwined with institutions, organizations, life styles, forms of production and consumption, etc., men become willing to sacrifice themselves and others for the works of their own hands, to transform their own creations into idols and to worship these idols. Furthermore, institutions generally resist change, and thus men who are fully committed to institutions are not free to anticipate change. The problem, then, for a society such as ours today, is whether men can rediscover the basic human and social values of our civilization, and withdraw their allegiance, not to say their worship, from those of their institutional (or ideological) values which have become obstructive.

There is one great difference between the past and the present that makes this an urgent question. The violent, unanticipated solution in our case will not lead to a bad peace as it did for Germany in 1918 or in 1945; it will not lead to some of our people—or some of the Russian people—being led away to captivity, as happened to the nations defeated by the Roman Em-

[1] This topic is admirably dealt with in Robert Heilbroner's *The Future as History,* Harper & Bros., New York, 1960.

pire; it will lead, most likely, to the physical destruction of most Americans and most Russians now living and to a barbaric, dehumanized, dictatorial regime for the survivors. This time the choice between violent-irrational, or anticipatory-rational behavior is a choice which will affect the human race and its cultural, if not its physical, survival.

Yet so far the chances that such rational-anticipatory action will occur are bleak. Not because there is no possibility for such an outcome in the realistic circumstances, but because on both sides there is a thought barrier built of clichés, ritualistic ideologies, and even a good deal of common craziness that prevents people —leaders and led—from seeing sanely and realistically what the facts are, from separating the facts from the fictions and, as a consequence, from recognizing alternative solutions to violence. Such rational anticipatory policy requires in the first place a critical examination of our assumptions about, among other things, the nature of communism, the future of the underdeveloped countries, the value of the deterrent for avoiding war. It requires also a serious examination of our own biases, and of certain semipathological forms of thinking which govern our behavior.

II) HISTORICAL ORIGINS
OF THE PRESENT CRISIS AND
PERSPECTIVES FOR THE FUTURE

After a process of about a thousand years, lasting from the beginning of the feudalization of the Roman Empire to the late Middle Ages, a period in which the European Continent was impregnated, through Christianity, with the ideas of Greek, Hebrew, and Arab thinking, Europe gave birth to a new culture. Western man discovered nature as an object of intellectual speculation and aesthetic enjoyment; he created a new science, which became—within a few centuries—the basis for a technique destined to transform nature and the practical life of man in a hitherto undreamed-of way; he discovered himself as an individual, endowed with almost unlimited energies and powers.

This new period engendered also a new hope for the improvement, or even, the perfection of man. The hope for man's perfection on this earth and for his capacity to build a "good society" is one of the most characteristic and unique features of occidental thought. It is a hope that had been held by the Old Testament prophets as well as by Greek philosophers. It had then been overshadowed—although never lost—by the transhistorical ideals of salvation and by the emphasis on man's substantial corruption in Christian thinking; it found new expression in the sixteenth- and seventeenth-century utopias and in the eighteenth- and nineteenth-century philosophical and political ideas.

Parallel to the blossoming of hope after the Renaissance and the Reformation went the explosive economic development of the West, the first industrial revolution. The organizational form it took was that of the system of capitalism, characterized by private property in the means of production, the existence of politically free wage earners, and the regulation of all economic activities by the principles of calculation and profit maximation. By 1913, industrial production increased seven times above its 1860 level, with almost all of it in Europe and North America. (Less than 10 per cent of world production took place outside of those two areas.)

Since the end of the First World War, mankind has entered into a new phase. The nature of the capitalistic mode of production has undergone profound changes. New productive forces (such as the use of oil, electricity, and atomic energy) and technical discoveries have increased material productivity many times over what it had been in the middle of the nineteenth century.

The new technical discoveries brought with them a new form of production. This was characterized by centralization of production in big plants, along with the dominant position of the big corporations; managerial bureaucracies, which head these corporations but do not own them; and a mode of production in which hundreds of thousands of manual and clerical workers co-operate smoothly, supported by strong trade unions, which often share the bureaucratic character of the big corporations. Centralization, bureaucratization, and manipulation are the characteristic features of the new mode of production.

The earlier period of industrial development, with its need to build up a heavy industry at the expense of the satisfaction of the material needs of the workers resulted in extreme poverty for the millions of men, women, and children who worked in factories during the nineteenth century. As a reaction to their misery, but also as an expression of human dignity and faith, the socialist movement spread over all of Europe and threatened to overthrow the old order and to replace it with one that would work for the benefit of the broad masses of the population.

The organization of labor combined with technical progress and the resulting increased productivity permitted the working class an ever-increasing share of the national product. The extreme dissatisfaction with the system that characterized the nineteenth century gave way to a spirit of co-operation within the capitalist system. A new partnership between industry and the workers, represented by trade unions and (with the exception of the United States) strong socialist parties took place. The trend toward violent revolutions ended in Europe after the First World War, except in the economically most backward country among the large powers—Russia.

While the gap between the "haves" and the "have-nots" has been narrowing considerably *within* the Western industrial countries (and slowly also in Soviet Russia), the gap between the "have countries" of Europe and North America and the "have-not countries" in Asia (with the exception of Japan), Africa, and Latin America is as wide as it ever was within one country, and is actually still widening. But while at the beginning of the twentieth century the colonial peoples accepted their exploitation and poverty, the middle of the same century is witnessing the full-scale revolution of the poor countries. Precisely as the workers within capitalism in the nineteenth century refused to continue believing that their fate had been ordained by divine or social law, so now the poor nations refuse to accept their poverty. They demand not only political freedom, but a standard of living approaching that of the Western world and rapid industrialization as a means to that goal. Two thirds of the human race are unwilling to accept a situation in which their standard of living is only from 10 to less than 5 per cent of that of the people of the richest country —the United States—which with 6 per cent of the world's population produces today about 40 per cent of the world's goods.

The colonial revolution was sparked by many factors, among them the weakening of Europe, militarily and economically, after the two World Wars in the first half of the twentieth century; the nationalistic and revolutionary ideology transmitted from nineteenth-century Europe and America, and the new modes of production and social organization, which raise the possibility of "catching up with the West" beyond a slogan into a realm of reality.

China, borrowing Communist ideology and economic and social methods from Soviet Russia, has become the first colonial country to make spectacular economic gains, beginning to transform herself into one of the great world powers and trying by example, persuasion, and economic help to become the leader of the colonial revolution in Asia, Africa, and Latin America.

While after 1923 the Soviet Union had definitely given up the hope for a workers' revolution in the West and, in fact, sought to contain all Western revolutionary movements since then, she had hoped for support from the nationalist revolutions in the East. Now, however, having herself become one of the "have" states, she feels threatened by the growing onslaught of the underdeveloped countries under China's leadership, and seeks an understanding with the United States, without, however, turning this understanding into an alliance against China.

Any description of the basic trends of Western history in the last four hundred years would be lacking in an essential element unless it took account of a profound spiritual change. While the influence of Christian theological thinking was waning from the seventeenth century onward, the same spiritual reality which was expressed earlier in the concepts of this theology found now a new expression in philosophical, historical, and political formulations. The philosophers of the eighteenth century were, as Carl Becker has pointed out, no less men of faith than were the theologians of the thirteenth century. They just expressed their experience in a different conceptual framework. With the explosive growth of wealth and technical capacities in the nineteenth century, there occurred a fundamental change in man's attitude. Not only, as Nietzsche put it, "God was dead," but the humanism that was common to the theologians of the thirteenth, and to the philosophers of the eighteenth centuries, slowly died too; the formulae and ideologies, both of religion and of humanism, continued to be used, but the authentic *experience* became increasingly thinner, to the point of unreality. It was as if man had become drunk with his own power, and had transformed material production, once a means to the end of a more dignified human life, into an end in itself.

Large-scale enterprise, state intervention, emphasis on control of—rather than ownership of—property in the means of production, are characteristic of all industrial systems today. The Western capitalist system, while it has many features of nineteenth-century capitalism, has incorporated enough of the new features to constitute a very different system from the former. The three forms of socialism current today, having broken much more drastically with the continuity of the former economic stage, show the new trends in different degrees and emphasis: a) Khrushchevism, a system of complete centralized planning and state ownership of industry and agriculture; b) Chinese communism, especially since 1958, a system of total mobilization of its most important capital asset, six hundred million people, and the complete manipulation of their physical and emotional energy and thoughts without regard to their individuality; c) humanistic socialism, which aims at the blending of a necessary minimum of centralization, state intervention, and bureaucracy with the possible maximum of decentralization, individualism, and freedom. This third type of socialism is represented by various forms from Scandinavia to Yugoslavia, Burma, and India.

On the basis of the recognition of these historical trends, the thesis which I want to present or to substantiate in the following pages is:

The Soviet Union, under Khrushchev's leadership, is a conservative, state-controlled, industrial managerialism, not a revolutionary system; she is interested in law and order and anxious to defend herself against the onslaught of the revolution of the "have-not" nations.

For this reason Khrushchev seeks an understanding with the United States, the ending of the cold war, and world disarmament. He neither needs nor wants war.

Khrushchev can not, however, give up his Communist-revolutionary ideology, nor can he turn against China, without undermining his own system. Hence he has to maneuver carefully to preserve his ideological hold on the Russian people and to defend himself against both his opponents within Russia and against China and her potential allies outside.

If he fails in his attempt to end the cold war with the West, he (or his successor) will be forced into a close alliance with China and into a policy which would leave little hope for peace.

The development of the former colonial peoples will not follow the capitalist development, because for psychological, social, and economic reasons this system is neither feasible nor attractive to them. The question is not whether they will join the communist *or* the capitalist systems. The real alternative is whether they will accept the Chinese or the Russian form of communism, thus becoming closely allied with either of these two countries, *or* whether they will adopt one of the various forms of democratic, decentralized socialism and become allied with the neutral bloc represented today by Tito, Nasser, and Nehru.

The United States is, therefore, confronted with the following alternative: either a continued fight against communism together with the continuation of the arms race—hence the probability of nuclear war—*or* a political understanding on the basis of the status quo with the Soviet Union, universal disarmament (with the inclusion of China), and the support of neutral democratic-socialist regimes in the colonial world. The latter solution would lead to a multi-polar world consisting of the Western bloc under United States and European leadership, the Soviet bloc under the leadership of the Soviet Union, China, the democratic socialist bloc under Yugoslav-Indian leadership, and the bloc of those other neutral nations outside of the above groups.

It is a fact that the two systems represented by Russia–China and by the United States–Western Europe are competing with each other in the world today. Any attempt of either one to defeat the other system through the use of military power will not only fail, but will lead to the destruction of both. There is only one way in which the United States can compete with communism: that is by demonstrating that it is possible to raise the standard of living in the underdeveloped countries to a degree comparable to that which totalitarian methods achieve, *without* using methods of coercive regimentation.

The existence of a multicentered world depends on the acceptance of the present status quo by all powers and on effective universal disarmament. The tension and suspicions of the nuclear arms race do not permit a political understanding; the unsettled political situation does not permit disarmament. Both disarmament *and* political understanding are necessary, if peace is to be preserved. However, in order to make these steps possible, several other steps are necessary: 1) Psychological disarmament, the ending of the hysterical hate and suspicion among the main protagonists that up to now have made realistic and objective thinking very difficult, if not impossible, on both sides. (Such psychological disarmament does not mean giving up political and philosophical convictions, nor the right to criticise other systems. On the contrary, it furthers such criticism and the assertion of one's own convictions, because they will not be tainted by hate and will not be used to foster a spirit of war.) 2) Massive economic aid—food, capital and technical assistance—to the underdeveloped countries, which will be possible only if, and when, the arms race ends. 3) Strengthening and reorganization of the United Nations in such a way that this organization has the capacity to supervise international disarmament and to organize large-scale economic assistance to the underdeveloped countries.

Related to this alternative in foreign policy is another one, hardly less important. In conquering poverty and achieving wealth, the United States, like the rest of the West (and Russia), has accepted a spirit of materialism under which production and consumption have become ends in themselves, rather than means to a more human, creative life. These and other institutional, secondary goals and values have become indistinguishable to most people from the primary aims of life. Quite aside from all dangers from without, our inner emptiness and deep-rooted lack of hope will eventually lead to the fall of Western civilization, unless a genuine renaissance of the Western spirit takes the place of the present complacency, resignation, and confusion. This renaissance must be precisely what the Renaissance of the fifteenth–seventeenth centuries was —an invigorating re-establishment of contact with the humanistic principles and aspirations of Western culture.

To sum up: what we are witnessing today is truly a world revolution in rapid advance, a revolution which began in the West four hundred years ago. It has led to a new system of production which at first made Europe and America the leaders of the world. It made the working masses in Europe beneficiaries of the system; and hence the revolution of the masses in Europe (with the exception of Russia) and in North America was peaceful. Now a new stage of the world revolution is developing, the revolution of the under-developed countries in Asia, Africa, and Latin America. The question is whether this revolution will also occur peacefully, which seems possible if the great industrial powers accept the historical trend and take the adequate anticipatory steps. If they do not do this, they will not stop the colonial revolution although they may beat it back for a brief historical instant. But, in this attempt to retard the colonial revolution, tensions will arise between the two blocs, pitted against each other with nuclear arms, that leave little hope for peace and the survival of democracy.

III) SANE VERSUS PATHOLOGICAL THINKING IN POLITICS

The idea that the Soviet Union is a conservative and not a revolutionary state, and the idea that the democratic socialist development of the underdeveloped countries need not be fought but should be welcomed by the United States—conflict with the assumptions most people make about these questions. They conflict not only intellectually, but also emotionally; they sound like heresies, nonsense, or subversion, according to the respective attitudes of the readers. Hence I believe it will be useful if I present some remarks on the psychological mechanism involved in these reactions to prepare the ground for a better understanding of what I have to say in the following chapters.

The understanding of one's own society and culture, just as the understanding of oneself, is the task of reason. But the obstacles reason has to overcome in the understanding of one's own society are no less than the formidable obstacles that, as Freud has shown, block the road to the understanding of oneself. These obstacles (Freud called them "resistance") lie by no means in the realm of intellectual shortcomings or lack of information. They lie in emotional factors which blunt or deform our instruments of thought to such an extent that they can become useless for the purpose of uncovering reality. Most people in any given society are unaware of the existence of this deformation. They see distortion only when it is a deviation from the attitude of the majority, but are convinced that majority opinions are sound and 'sane'.[2] Yet this is not so. Just as there is a *folie à deux*, there is insanity of millions, and consensus in error does not transform error into truth. To later generations, years after the outbreak of mass insanity, the insane character of such thinking, even though it was shared by almost everybody may be clear; thus some of the more extreme psychic reac-

[2] Cf. my detailed examination of this problem in *The Sane Society*, Rinehart & Co., Inc., New York, 1955.

tions to the Black Death in the Middle Ages, the witch hunting at the time of the Counter Reformation, the religious hatred in England in the seventeenth century, the hatred against the Huns during the First World War, appear to be pathological manifestations many years later. But usually there is little awareness of the pathological character of much that passes for "thinking" while it is occurring. I shall outline in the following pages some of the most important forms of pathological thinking about politics and foreign affairs, since it is of vital importance that we have an unspoiled instrument with which to understand contemporary political events.

I shall begin with the description of one of the more extreme forms of pathological thinking, *paranoid* thinking. The case of an individual suffering from paranoic delusions is clear to the psychiatrist and to most laymen as well. The man who tells us that everybody is "after him," that his colleagues, his friends, and even his wife are conspiring to murder him is recognized by most as being insane. On what basis? Quite obviously not because the accusations he makes are logically *impossible*. It could be that his enemies, his acquaintances, and even his family have united to destroy him; in fact such things have happened. We can not truthfully answer the unfortunate patient and say that what he assumes is not *possible*. We can only argue that it is very *unlikely;* that it is unlikely due to the infrequency of such events in general and the character of his wife and friends in particular.

Yet we shall not convince the patient. For him, reality is based on logical possibility not on probability. This attitude is exactly the basis of his illness. His contact with reality rests on the small basis of its compatibility with the laws of logical thinking, and does not require the examination of realistic *probability*. It does not require it because the paranoic is not capable of making this examination. As with every psychotic patient, his contact with reality is exceedingly thin and brittle. Reality, for him, is mainly what exists within himself, his own emotions, fears, and desires. The world outside is the mirror or the symbolic representation of his inner world.

But, in contrast to the schizophrenic person, many paranoid persons have preserved one aspect of sane thinking: the requirement of logical possibility. They have merely relinquished the other, the aspect of realistic probability. If only possibility is required as a condition for truth, it is easy to achieve certainty. If, on the other hand, probability is required, there are relatively few things to be certain of. This is indeed what makes paranoid thinking so "attractive" in spite of the suffering it causes. It saves man from doubt. It guarantees a sense of certainty, which transcends most insights to which sane thinking can lead.

It is easy for people to recognize paranoid thinking in the individual case of a paranoid psychotic. But to recognize paranoid thinking when it is shared by millions of other people and approved by the authorities who lead them, is more difficult. A case in point is the conventional thinking about Russia. Most Americans today think about Russia in a paranoid fashion; namely, they ask what is *possible* rather than what is *probable*. Indeed, it is possible that Khrushchev wants to conquer us by force. It is possible that he makes peace proposals in order to make us unaware of the danger. It is also possible that his whole argument with the Chinese Communists about coexistence is nothing but a trick to make us believe that he wants peace in order to all the better surprise us. If we think only of *possibilities,* then indeed there is no chance for realistic and sensible political action.

Sane thinking means not only to think of possibilities, which in fact are always relatively easy to recognize, but to think also of probabilities. That means to examine the realistic situations, and to predict to some extent an opponent's probable action by means of an analysis of all the factors and motivations that influence his behavior. To make this point perfectly clear, I want to state that my emphasis on sane versus paranoid thinking does not imply a judgment that the Russians *might* not have all the sinister and deceptive plans just mentioned. Instead, it insists we must conduct a thorough and dispassionate examination of the facts and that logical possibility as such proves nothing and means little.

Another pathological mechanism which threatens realistic and effective political thinking is that of *projection.* Everyone is familiar with this mechanism in its cruder forms when it appears in individual cases. Everybody knows the hostile and destructive person who accuses everybody else of being hostile and pictures himself as being innocent and victimized. There are thousands of marriages that continue to exist on the basis of this projective mechanism. Each of the partners accuses the other of what in reality is his own problem, and hence succeeds in being entirely occupied with the problem of his partner instead of facing his own. Again what is easily seen in individual cases is not seen when the same projective mechanism is shared by millions and supported by their leaders. For example, during the First World War, the peoples in the allied countries believed that the Germans were vile Huns, killing innocent babies and that they were the true personification of all evil to the extent that even the music of Bach and Beethoven became a part of the Devil's territory. On the other hand the accusers of the Huns were fighting only for the noblest purposes, for freedom, for peace, for democracy, and so on. The Germans, strangely enough, believed exactly the same things about the allies.

What is the result? The enemy appears as the embodiment of all evil because all evil that I feel in myself is projected on to him. Logically, after this has happened, I consider myself as the embodiment of all good since the evil has been transferred to the other side. The result is indignation and hatred against the enemy and uncritical, narcissistic self-glorification. This can create a mood of common mania and shared passion of hate. Nevertheless, it is pathological thinking, dangerous when it leads to war and deadly when war means destruction.

Our attitudes toward communism, the Soviet Union, and Communist China are, to a considerable extent, demonstrations of projective thinking. Indeed, the Stalinist terror system was inhuman, cruel, and revolting, although no more so than the terror in a number of countries that we call free—no more so, for instance, than was the terror of Trujillo or Batista.

I do not mention non-communist cruelty or callousness as being extenuating factors in judging the Stalin regime, because obviously cruelties and inhumanities do not cancel out each other. I mention them to show that the indignation of many people against Stalin is not as genuine as they believe it to be. If it were, they would feel just as indignant about other cases of cruelty and callousness, whether the perpetrators happen to be their political enemies or not. But more than that, *the Stalin regime has gone.* Russia is now a conservative police regime, which is by no means a desirable thing if one cherishes freedom and individuality, but which also should not arouse the kind of deep human indignation that the Stalinist system merited. It is fortunate that the Russian regime has changed from cruel terrorism to the methods of a conservative police state. It also shows a lack of sincerity in those lovers of freedom who are most vocal in their hatred of the Soviet Union that they seem hardly to be aware of the considerable change that has occurred.

Many still continue to believe that communism is the epitome of evil, and that we, the free world, including such allies as Franco, are the personification of all that is good. The result is the narcissistic and unrealistic picture of the West as the fighter for good, for freedom, and for humanity, and of communism as the enemy of all that is human and decent. The Communist Chinese, especially in their way of looking at the West, follow the same mechanism.

If projection is mixed with paranoid thinking, as is the case during a war and also in the "cold war," we have, indeed, a dangerously explosive psychological mixture, which prevents sane and anticipatory thinking.

This discussion of pathological thinking would remain incomplete were we not to consider one more type of pathology that plays a great role in political thought—that of *fanaticism*. What is a fanatic? How can we recognize him? There is a tendency today, when genuine conviction has become so rare, to call "fanatic" anyone who has a deep faith in a spiritual or scientific conviction that differs radically from the opinions of others, and has not yet been proven. If this were so, then indeed, the greatest and most courageous men —Buddha, Isaiah, Socrates, Jesus, Galileo, Darwin, Marx, Freud, Einstein—would all have been "fanatics."

The question of who is a fanatic can often not be answered by judging the *contents* of an assertion. For instance, faith in man and in his potentialities can not be *proven* intellectually, although it can be deeply rooted in the authentic experience of the believer. Again, in scientific thought, there is often quite a distance from the stage of hypothesis formation to valid proof, and the scientist needs to have faith in his thinking, until he can arrive at the stage of proof. True enough, there are many assertions that are clearly in contrast to the laws of rational thought, and anyone who holds an unshakable belief in them may be correctly called a fanatic. But often it is not easy to decide what is irrational and what is not, and neither "proof" nor general agreement are sufficient criteria.

In fact, it is easier to recognize the fanatic by some qualities in his personality rather than by the contents of his convictions. The most important—and usually an observable—personal quality in the fanatic is a kind of "cold fire," a passion which at the same time has no warmth. The fanatic is unrelated to the world outside himself; he is not concerned with anybody or anything —even though he may proclaim his concern as an important part of his "faith." The cold glitter in his eyes often tells us more about the fanatical quality of his ideas than the apparent "unreasonableness" of the ideas themselves.

Speaking in a more theoretical vein, the fanatic can be described as a highly narcissistic person who is disengaged from the world outside. He does not really feel anything since authentic feeling is always the result of the interrelation between oneself *and* the world. The fanatic's pathology is similar to that of a depressed person who suffers not from sadness (which would be a relief) but from the incapacity to feel anything. The fanatic is different from the depressed person (and in some ways similar to the manic) inasmuch as he has found a way out of acute depression. He has built for himself an idol, an absolute, to which he surrenders completely but of which he also makes himself a part. He then acts, thinks, and feels in the name of his idol, or rather, he has the illusion of "feeling," of inner excitement, while he has no *authentic* feeling. He lives in a state of narcissistic excitement since he has drowned the feeling of his isolation and emptiness in a total submission to the idol and in the simultaneous deification of his own ego, which he has made part of the idol. He is passionate in his idolatric submission and in his grandiosity; yet cold in his inability for genuine relatedness and feeling. His attitude may be described symbolically as "burning ice." He will be particularly deceptive to others if the content of his idol is love, brotherliness, God, salvation, the country, the race, honor, etc., rather than frank destructiveness, hostility, or overt desire for conquest. But, as far as human reality is concerned, it makes little difference what the nature of the idol is. Fanaticism is always the result of the incapacity for authentic relatedness. The fanatic is so seductive, and hence so dangerous politically, because he *seems* to feel so intensely and to be so convinced. Since we all long for certainty and passionate experience, is it surprising that the fanatic succeeds in attracting so many with his counterfeit faith and feelings?

Paranoid, projective and fanatical political thinking are all truly pathological forms of thought processes, different from pathology in the conventional sense only by the fact that political thoughts are shared by a larger group of people and not restricted to one or two individuals. These pathological forms of thinking, however, are not the only ones that block the way to the proper grasp of political reality. There are other forms of thinking, which should perhaps not be called pathological, yet which are equally dangerous, maybe only because they are more common. I refer especially to unauthentic, automaton-thinking. The process is simple: I believe something to be true, not because I have arrived at the thought by my own thinking, based on my own observation and experience, but because it has been "suggested" to me. In automaton-thinking I may be under the illusion that my thoughts are my own when actually I have adopted them because they have been presented by sources that carry authority in one form or another.

All of modern thought manipulation, whether it is in commercial advertising or in political propaganda, makes use of the suggestive-hypnoid techniques which produce thoughts and feelings in people without making them aware that "their" thoughts are not their own. The art of brain-washing that the Chinese seem to have brought to a certain perfection is actually only a more extreme form of this hypnoid suggestion. With increasing skill in suggestive techniques, authentic thinking becomes more and more replaced by automaton-thinking, yet the great illusion of the voluntary and spontaneous character of our thoughts is kept alive.

It is quite remarkable how readily groups recognize the unauthentic character of thought in opponents but not in themselves. American travelers, for instance, returning from the Soviet Union, report their impressions about the uniformity of political thinking in Russia. Everybody seems to ask the same questions, from "What about lynchings in the South?" to "Why does the United States need so many military bases surrounding the Soviet Union if the Americans have peaceful intentions?"

What the travelers to Russia who report on the uniformity of opinion there are not aware of is that public opinion in the United States is hardly less uniform. Most Americans take for granted a number of clichés such as that the Russians want to conquer the world for revolutionary communism, that because they do not believe in God they have no concept of morality similar to our own, and so on. Furthermore, in the United States—to what extent this is true in the Soviet Union I can of course not even try to guess—the cliché opinions are by no means restricted only to the lower ranks of the people. They are also held by many of those who as practical politicians, intellectuals, and newspaper and radio commentators, etc., have a share in the formulation of practical policy and in the shaping of public opinion.

This kind of unauthentic, automaton thinking results in *"doublethink,"* which George Orwell has so brilliantly described as the logic of totalitarian thought. "Doublethink," he says in his book *1984,*[3] *"means the power of holding two contradictory beliefs in one's mind, and accepting both of them."* We are familiar with the Russian *doublethink.* Countries like Hungary and East Germany, whose governments clearly rule against the will of the vast majority of the population, are called "people's democracies." A hierarchical class society built along rigid lines of economic, social and political inequality is called a "classless society." A system in which the power of the state has been increasing for the last forty years is said to lead to the "withering away of the State." But *doublethink* is by no means only a Soviet phenomenon. We in the West call dictatorships "part of the free world" if they are anti-Russian. Thus dictators like Syngman Rhee, Chiang Kai-

[3] Latest edition by The New American Library, 1961, with an afterword by E. Fromm.

shek, Franco, Salazar, Batista, to mention only a few, were acclaimed as fighters for freedom and democracy, and the truth about their regimes was suppressed or distorted. Besides that, we permitted men like Chiang, Rhee, and Adenauer to influence and, sometimes modify, American foreign policy. The American public is misinformed about Korea, Formosa, Laos, the Congo, and Germany to a degree that is in flagrant contrast to our picture of ourselves as having a free press and an informed public.[4] We call it subversion when the Russians make anti-American propaganda, but Radio Free Europe's broadcasts to the Eastern European countries are *not* subversive. We proclaim our respect for the independence of all small countries, but we support the overthrow of the Guatemalan and the Cuban governments. We are horrified at the Russian terror in Hungary, but not at the French terror in Algeria.

Pathological thinking and *doublethink* are not only sick and inhuman, but they endanger our very survival. In a situation where errors in judgment can bring about catastrophic consequences we can not afford to indulge in pathological or cliché-ridden forms of thinking. The clearest and most realistic thought about the world situation, especially with regard to the conflict between the Soviet bloc and the Western bloc becomes a matter of vital necessity. Today certain opinions are held with pride as being "realistic," when they actually are as fantastic and unrealistic as are some of the Pollyannish illusions that they attack. It is a peculiar frailty of

[4] For substantiation of these statements I refer the reader to the recent book by William J. Lederer, *A Nation of Sheep*, W. W. Norton, Inc., New York, 1961, who discusses in detail "The Laos Fraud," "What we aren't told about Formosa," "What we aren't told about Korea," and the role of "misinformation," "publicity," and "secrecy" in the United States government.

human reactions that many are prone to believe that a cynical, "tough" perspective is more likely to be "realistic" than a more objective, complex, and constructive one. Apparently many people think that it takes a strong and courageous man to see things simply and without too many complexities, or to risk catastrophe without blinking.[5] They forget that it often takes fanatical, self-righteous, and ignorant men to confuse what C. W. Mills has so rightly called "crackpot realism" with a rational appreciation of reality.

Paranoid, projective, fanatical, and automaton thinking are various forms of thought processes, which are all rooted in the same basic phenomenon—in the fact that the human race has not arrived yet at the level of development expressed in the great humanist religions and philosophies that came to life in India, China, Palestine, Persia, and Greece from 1500 B.C. to the time of Christ. While most people *think* in terms of these religious systems and of their nontheological philosophical successors, they are still emotionally on an archaic, irrational level, not different from the one that existed before the ideas of Buddhism, Judaism, and Christianity had been proclaimed. We still worship idols. We do not call them Baal or Astarte but we worship and submit to our idols under different names.

Technically and intellectually we are living in an

---

[5] It seems, for instance, that the admiration with which Herman Kahn's recent book *On Thermonuclear War,* Princeton University Press, Princeton, 1960, has been received in many quarters is due precisely to this mechanism. Anyone who can present a "budget" of from 5 to 160 million fatalities in a nuclear war without shrinking, who can reassure us that 60 million killed will not seriously diminish the survivors' pleasure in living, must be strong and "realistic." Not many then observe how flimsy and unrealistic many of his thoughts and "proofs" are.

atomic age; emotionally we are still living in the Stone Age. We feel superior to the Aztecs who on a feast day sacrificed 20,000 men to their gods, in the belief this would keep the universe in its proper course. We sacrifice millions of men for various goals that *we* think are noble and we justify the slaughter. But the facts are the same, only the rationalizations are different. Man, in spite of all his intellectual and technical progress, is still caught in the idol worship of blood ties, property, and institutions. His reason is still governed by irrational passions. He has still not experienced what it is to be fully human. We still have a double standard of values for judging our own and outside groups. The history of civilized man until now is really very short, comparable to less than an hour in a human life. It is not amazing or discouraging that we have still not reached maturity. Those who believe in man's capacity to become what he potentially is would have no need to be alarmed were it not that the discrepancy between emotional and intellectual-technical development has reached such proportions now that we are threatened with extinction or a new barbarism. This time only a fundamental and authentic change will save us.

Yet we so little know how to accomplish this change —and the times are so pressing. One approach is to speak the *truth*. We must penetrate the net of rationalizations, self-delusions, and doublethink. We must be objective and see the world and ourselves realistically and undistorted by narcissism and xenophobia. Freedom exists only where there is reason and truth. Archaic tribalism and idolatry flourish where the voice of reason is silent. Does it not follow that to know the truth about the facts of foreign policy is of vital importance for the preservation of freedom and of peace?

The nature of the Soviet system

The Soviet system is a mythical entity to most Americans; probably not any less mythical than the capitalist system is to most Russians. While the Russians see capitalism as a system of exploited wage slaves obeying the whip of Wall Street bosses, Americans see Russia as led by men who are a blend of Lenin and Hitler, bent on subjugating the rest of the world by force or trickery. Since our whole foreign policy is based on the idea that the Soviet Union wants to conquer the world by force, it is of the utmost importance to examine the facts and to have a clear and realistic picture of the nature of the Soviet system. This task is all the more difficult because the nature of the Soviet system changed completely between 1917 and the present time. It changed from a revolutionary system, considering itself the center and the promoter of Communist revolutions in Europe and eventually throughout the whole world, to a conservative, industrial class society run along lines in many respects similar to the development of the "capitalistic" states of the West.

This change, however, was never marked by any official break in the continuity, because many basic features such as the nationalization of the means of production and the idea of a planned economy have remained the same. But much more confusing than the continuity of certain economic patterns is the continuity of the *ideology*. For reasons that will be discussed later, Stalin and then Khrushchev have religiously stuck to the "Marxist-Leninist" formulations, and continued to speak the language of 1848 or 1917, although representing a system which is the very opposite of what revolutionaries like Marx and Lenin envisaged.

Actually we should be better able to recognize the difference between ritualized ideological formulae and realities. Are we not ourselves caught in a similar discrepancy when we talk of "individual initiative" in a society of the "organization man," or of a "God-fearing society" when in reality we care mainly about money, comfort, health and education, and very little about God? However—and this makes the recognition of reality all the more confusing—neither the Russians nor we are liars. Both sides are convinced that they are telling the truth, and they approach each other with the common conviction that their own and, even to some extent, their opponent's ideologies represent realities.

It is my intention in this chapter to break through the existing clichés and to arrive at a realistic appreciation of the existing Soviet system. I will compare the brief revolutionary period, which lasted from 1917 to 1922, with the transformation of that system into the totalitarian managerialism of Stalin and Khrushchev. I will attempt to substantiate in detail the nonsocialist and nonrevolutionary character of today's Soviet system and furthermore to show that since Stalin's ascendancy the Soviet rulers have never aimed at a Communist revolution in the West but have used the Communist parties only as instruments for the support of Soviet foreign policy.

I) THE REVOLUTION—A HOPE THAT FAILED

The middle of the nineteenth century was a time of

socialist hope; this hope was based on the miraculous progress of science and its effect on industrial production, on the success of the middle-class revolutions of 1789, 1830, 1848, on the mounting protests of the workers, and on the spread of socialist ideas. Marx and Engels, like many other socialists, were convinced that the time was near in which the great revolution would occur and that shortly a new epoch in human history would begin, that there was every prospect, as Engels put it, "of turning the revolution of the minority" [as were all previous revolutions] "into a revolution of the majority" [as he visualized the socialist revolution]. But at the end of the century Engels had to admit: "History has proved us, and all who thought like us, wrong. It has made it clear that the state of economic development of the continent at that time was not, by a long way, ripe for the elimination of capitalist production . . ."[1]

The First World War marked a decisive change in the history of socialism. It marked the collapse of two of its most significant aims, internationalism and peace. With the beginning of the war, each socialist party took the side of its own government and fought the other socialists in the name of "freedom." This moral debacle of socialism was not so much due to the personal betrayal of some leaders as to the change in general economic and political conditions. The naked and ruthless exploitation of the workers which had existed in the nineteenth century had slowly given way to the participation of the working class in the economic gains

[1] F. Engels, Introduction (1895) to K. Marx, *The Class Struggles in France 1848 to 1850*, K. Marx and F. Engels, *Selected Works*, Foreign Languages Publishing House, Moscow, 1955, Vol. I, p. 125.

of their respective countries. Capitalism, instead of being unable to function because of its own inner contradictions, as Marx had predicted, proved to be a going concern, much more capable of coping with crises and difficulties than the radical revolutionaries had expected.[2]

The very success of capitalism led to a new interpretation of socialism. While Marx's and Engels's vision was that of a new form of society *transcending* that of capitalism, a society which would be the full realization of humanism and individualism, socialism began now to be interpreted by most of its adherents as a movement for the economic and political rise of the working class *within* the capitalist system. While Marxist socialism in the nineteenth century was the most significant spiritual and moral movement of the century, antipositivistic and antimaterialistic in its essence, it was slowly transformed into a purely political movement with essentially economic aims even though the older moral goals never entirely disappeared. The interpretation of socialism in terms of the categories of capitalism led to a new policy for the socialist parties, the aim of which was the welfare state rather than the fulfillment of the messianic hopes held by the founders of socialism.

The war of 1914, that senseless slaughter of millions of people of all nations for the sake of certain economic advantages, led to the resurgence, in a new and vital form, of the older socialist attitude against war and nationalism. Radical socialists in all countries felt a profound indignation at the war, and they became the

[2] These factors furnished the basis for the development of the "revisionist" wing in the socialist movement, whose main theoretical exponent was E. Bernstein, in the years before the First World War.

leaders of revolutionary movements in Russia, Germany, and France. In fact, the radicalization of the socialist movement was closely connected with the Zimmerwald movement, the attempt of internationalist socialists to end the war.

The February revolution in Russia gave new impetus to these revolutionary leaders. Originally Lenin, in accordance with Marx's theory, had believed that a socialist revolution could be successful only within a highly developed, capitalist economy like Germany. He had thought it necessary that a less-developed country like Russia had to complete its bourgeois revolution before moving forward to a socialist revolution.[3] For the same reason the majority of the Communist Central Committee was at first opposed to the seizure of power in 1917, but the increasing protest of the peasant-soldiers against the war coupled with the incapacity of the Czarist government and its revolutionary successors to end the war and to reorganize the Russian economy pushed Lenin into the October revolution. Lenin's and Trotsky's hopes were fastened on a German revolution, which both were sure would happen in a short while. They signed the peace treaty of Brest-Litovsk with Imperial Germany in the expectation that the German revolution would soon break out and invalidate the peace treaty. If a highly industrial Germany became a Soviet state and fused with mainly agricultural Russia, then, so they reasoned following Marxist theory, a socialist, German-Russian Soviet system would have a good chance to survive and to flourish. Like Marx and Engels in the middle

[3] Edward H. Carr, *The Bolshevik Revolution 1917–1923*, The Macmillan Co., New York, 1951, Vol. II, p. 270.

of the nineteenth century, Lenin and Trotsky seventy
years later believed for a short while that the socialist
"kingdom is near," and that they would lay the foundations for a truly socialist society.

Lenin's hope had its peaks and its valleys; 1917 and
1918 represented the first peak. Ten days after the
October revolution he declared: "We shall march
firmly and unswervingly to the victory of socialism
which will be sealed by the leading workers of the most
civilized countries and give to the people solid peace
and deliverance from all oppression and all exploitation."[4] When after the outbreak of the German revo-

---

[4] Quoted by Edward H. Carr, *The Bolshevik Revolution
1917–1923*, The Macmillan Co., New York, 1951, Vol. I,
p. 107. Carr's work is an excellently documented and objective historical analysis of the whole development of the Russian revolution from 1917 to 1923. Cf. furthermore for the
early history of the Russian-American relations after the
revolution George Kennan's penetrating two volumes, *Russia Leaves the War*, and *The Decision to Intervene*, Princeton University Press, Princeton, 1956 and 1958, and for the
period until 1941 the same author's *Soviet Foreign Policy
1917–1941*, D. van Nostrand Co. Inc., Princeton, 1960. For
the later periods of Russian communism, cf. David J. Dallin,
Soviet Foreign Policy After Stalin, J. B. Lippincott Co.,
Philadelphia, 1961. W. W. Rostow, *The Dynamics of Soviet
Society*, A Mentor Book, 1952. Alvin Z. Rubinstein, *The
Foreign Policy of the Soviet Union*, Random House, New
York, 1960. Robert V. Daniels, *The Conscience of the
Revolution*, Harvard University Press, Cambridge, 1960.
Louis Fischer, *The Soviets in World Affairs*, Vintage Books,
New York, 1951 and 1960 and the same author's *Russia,
America and the World*, Harper & Bros., New York, 1960,
Isaac Deutscher, *Stalin*, Vintage Books, New York, 1960
and the same author's first two volumes of his Trotsky
biography, *The Prophet Armed*, and *The Prophet Un-*

lution in November 1918, the new German government showed great reluctance to enter into diplomatic relations with Russia and when the German workers did not seem to follow the Russian example, doubts began to enter Lenin's and Trotsky's minds. In 1919 the Soviet revolutions in Bavaria and Hungary gave rise to new hopes, only to be dashed shortly by the defeat of these revolutions. The summer and fall of 1920, when the Russian civil war was moving toward its end and the Red Army stood at the gates of Warsaw, witnessed the peak of the prestige of the Comintern and of the Communist hopes for world revolution.[5] The second Congress of the Comintern, 1920, was held in a mood of high revolutionary enthusiasm. Yet, only a short time after, with the defeat of the Red Army before Warsaw and the failure of the Polish workers to rise, everything changed dramatically. The revolutionary hopes received a shock from which they never recovered.

---

armed, Oxford University Press, London, 1959. L. Trotsky's *Stalin,* Harper & Bros., 1946. Zbigniew K. Brzezinski, *The Soviet Bloc,* Harvard University Press, Cambridge, 1960. David Granick, *The Red Executive,* Doubleday, New York, 1960. H. L. Boorman, A. Eckstein, Ph. Mosely, B. Schwartz, *Moscow-Peking Axis,* Harper & Bros., 1957, Herbert Marcuse, *Soviet Marxism,* Columbia University Press, New York, 1958. Edward Kardely, *Socialism and War,* Beograd, 1960. Furthermore, the very informative papers collected in *The Papers submitted by Panelists appearing before the Joint Economic Committee, Congress of the U.S.,* U. S. Government Printing Office, Washington 1959 (quoted in the following pages as *Congr. Committee Papers*) and various papers in *Foreign Affairs, Problems of Communism,* and *Soviet Quarterly.*

[5] Cf. E. H. Carr, Vol. III, p. 165 ff.

Lenin, in ordering the march on Warsaw, after the successful defense against the Polish attack, had yielded to his frantic hope for world revolution, this time being less realistic than Trotsky, who (with Tukhachevski) had advised against the Warsaw offensive. Once more history proved that the revolutionaries had been wrong in their estimates of the revolutionary possibilities. Lenin recognized the defeat; he admitted that Western capitalism still had a much greater vitality than he had expected and he initiated and organized the retreat in order to save what could be saved from the debacle. He started the NEP, the reintroduction of capitalism in large sectors of the Russian economy, he tried to persuade foreign capitalists to invest capital in "concessions" within the Soviet Union, he tried to arrive at a peaceful understanding with the great Western powers and, at the same time, he suppressed by force the movement of the Kronstadt sailors, directed against what they felt to be the betrayal of the revolution.

I will resist the temptation to discuss here the errors of Lenin and Trotsky, and the question of to what extent they had been following Marx's teachings. Suffice it to say that Lenin's concept that the true interest of the working class resided in an élite of leaders, and not in the majority of workers, was not Marx's; in fact, it was opposed by Trotsky during the many years of differences between him and Lenin before the outbreak of the First World War as it was opposed by Rosa Luxemburg, the most unwavering and clearsighted of Marxist revolutionary leaders until her assassination by German soldiers in 1919. Lenin did not see what Rosa Luxemburg and many others saw, that the centralized, bureaucratic system in which an élite ruled *for* the workers had to end up in a system in which it would rule *over* the workers and extinguish whatever was left of socialism in Russia. But whatever the differences between Marx and Lenin were, the fact is that for the second time the great hope had failed. This time, however, the failure found Lenin and Trotsky in power, confronted with the historical dilemma of how to guide a socialist revolution in a country that did not have the objective conditions for a socialist society. They were spared the problem of having to solve this dilemma. Lenin, after a first stroke in 1922 which incapacitated him increasingly, died in January 1924; Trotsky was driven from power a few years later; Stalin, with whom Lenin had broken off all personal relations in the last months before his death, took over.

Lenin's death and Trotsky's defeat only underscored the end of the period of revolutionary movements all over Europe and of hopes for a new socialist order. After 1919 the revolution was on the retreat, and by 1923 there was no longer any doubt about its failure.

II) STALIN'S TRANSFORMATION OF
THE COMMUNIST, INTO
A MANAGERIAL REVOLUTION

Stalin, a shrewd, cynical opportunist with an insatiable lust for personal power, drew the consequences of the failure. Given his personality, socialism could never have meant for him the human vision of Marx or Engels, and hence he had no scruples in introducing the enforced industrialization of Russia under the name of "socialism in one country." This formula was only the transparent cover for the goal to be achieved—the building of a totalitarian state managerialism in Russia,[6,7] and the rapid capital accumulation (and mobilization of human energy) necessary for this goal.

Stalin liquidated the socialist revolution in the name of "socialism." He used terror to enforce acceptance of the material deprivations which resulted from the rapid build-up of basic industries at the expense of the production of consumer goods; furthermore, the terror served to create a new *work morale* by mobilizing the energies of an essentially agrarian population and forcing them to work at the pace necessary for this rapid industrial expansion. He used terror probably far beyond what was necessary for the achievement of his economic program because he was possessed by an extraordinary thirst for power, a paranoid suspicion of rivals, and a pathological pleasure in revenge.[8]

If a highly industrialized, centralized Russian state managerialism was Stalin's aim, he certainly could not

[6] While it is true that Lenin and Trotsky too believed that after the failure of the German revolution Russia's hope lay in rapid industrialization, their socialist vision was genuine, and hence they would never have called the evolving system "socialism." Lenin clearly stated in April 1917 that the introduction of socialism was not the immediate task, which was merely the transition of control over production and distribution to the Soviets of workers' deputies.

[7] I use the term industrial "state managerialism" as the one which avoids certain ambiguities and difficulties in the term "state capitalism". In the later discussion it will be made clearer which elements of capitalism are to be found in the Stalinist system and what are the essential differences. Another term which could be used is the one coined by one of the leading German Marxist economists, R. Hilferding, "totalitarian state economy."

[8] It will be described later how he transformed the Communist movement into a tool of Russian foreign policy.

have said so. Terror alone, even the most extreme terror, would not have sufficed to force the masses into co-operation had not Stalin been able also to influence men's minds and thoughts. He could, of course, have made a complete about-face, staging an ideological counterrevolution employing a fascist-nationalist ideology. Thus he might have had the ideological means which would have led to similar results. Stalin did not choose this course, and hence there was nothing left for him to do but to use the only ideology which had any influence on the masses at that time—that of communism and world revolution. Religion had been depreciated by the Communist Party; nationalism had been depreciated; "Marxism-Leninism" was the only prestigeful ideology left. And not only this, but the figures of Marx, Engels, and Lenin had a charismatic appeal for the Russian people and Stalin used this appeal by presenting himself as their legitimate successor. In order to perpetrate the great historical fraud, Stalin had to get rid of Trotsky and eventually to exterminate almost all the old Bolsheviks to have the way completely free for his transformation of the socialist goal into one of a reactionary state managerialism. He had to rewrite history in order to wipe out even the memory of the old revolutionaries and their ideas. Maybe, unconsciously, he feared and suspected the old revolutionaries in his paranoid fashion, because he felt guilty of having betrayed the ideals of which they were the symbols.

Stalin succeeded in his goal, which was not world revolution but an industrialized Russia that should become the strongest industrial power in Europe, if not in the whole world. The economic success of his method of totalitarian state planning later continued with some changes by Malenkov and Khrushchev, is no longer a matter of dispute. "The Soviet system of centralized direction has proved itself to be more or less the peer of the market economy, as exemplified by the United States."[9] This judgment is borne out by the Russian industrial growth.[10] While the estimates of various American economists vary somewhat, the differences are relatively small. Bornstein estimates the annual rate of growth of gross national product from 1950 to 1958 in the Soviet Union at 6.5–7.5 per cent and for the United States in the same period at 2.9 per cent.[11] Kaplan-Moorsteen estimate the Russian industrial rate of growth for the same period as being 9.2 per cent. Campbell estimates the present rate of growth in the Soviet Union at 6 per cent.[12] If one considers the Russian annual rate of growth since 1913, that is to say for the period including the destruction of the First World War and the Civil War, the figures are, of course, quite different. They are, according to Nutter, for *civilian* industrial output from 1913 to 1955 only 4.2 per cent, while the rate of growth for the last forty years of the Czarist period was 5.3

[9] Warren S. Nutter, The Structure and Growth of Soviet Industry, A Comparison with the United States, *Congr. Committee Papers*, p. 118.

[10] Cf. the papers by W. Nutter, l.c.; furthermore, Morris Bornstein, "National Income and Product, A Comparison of Soviet and United States National Product," *Congr. Committee Papers;* W. W. Rostow, "Summary and Policy Implication," *Congr. Committee Papers* and Norman E. Kaplan and Richard H. Moorsteen, "An Index of Soviet Industrial Output," *The American Economic Review*, June 1960, pp. 295–318.

[11] Morris Bornstein, l.c. p. 391.

[12] Robert W. Campbell, *Soviet Economic Power*, Houghton Mifflin Co., Boston, 1960, p. 51.

per cent.[13] But between 1928 and 1940 (that is to say, in a period of peace) the Soviet rate was 8.3 per cent and between 1950 and 1955 9.0 per cent, more or less twice the United States rate during the same time,[14,15] and somewhat less than twice that of the Czarist rate. Nutter estimates that if one looks to the immediate future—"it seems reasonably certain that industrial growth will proceed more rapidly in the Soviet Union than in the United States, in the absence of radical institutional changes in either country," while, "it is more doubtful that industrial growth in the Soviet Union will be faster than in rapidly expanding Western economies, such as Western Germany, France and Japan."[16] Nutter doubts, however, that in the long run the Soviet system will generate a more rapid growth than the private enterprise system. In contrast to industrial production, Russian agricultural production has been lagging far behind the planned figures and still constitutes one of the difficult problems of the Russian system.

As far as *consumption* is concerned, the annual growth, taking in account the growth in population, is estimated at about 5 per cent, with a recent rise in consumption among peasants.[17] "In terms of food and

[13] I fail to see that the factor of considerable foreign capital investments in the Czarist economy is taken into account in these comparisons. Russia, as well as later China, had to finance her economy almost entirely with her own savings.

[14] W. Nutter, l.c. p. 100.

[15] In the paper by Kaplan-Moorsteen the rate of growth estimates of various American economists are compared.

[16] W. Nutter, l.c. p. 119.

[17] Lynn Turgeon, Levels of Living, Wages and Prices in the Soviet and United States Economies, *Congr. Committee Papers*, p. 319 ff.

clothing," Turgeon concludes, "the Soviet stands the best chance of overtaking our level of living," while the United States is far ahead in automobiles and other durable consumer goods, and in expenditures for services and travel.[18]

Stalin laid the foundations for a new, industrialized Russia. He transformed, within less than thirty years, the economically most backward of the great European nations into an industrial system that soon would become the economically most advanced and prosperous, second only to the United States. He achieved this goal through the ruthless destruction of human lives and happiness, through the cynical falsification of socialist ideas, and through an inhumanity which, together with that of Hitler, corroded the sense of humanity in the rest of the world. Yet apart from the question whether this goal could have been achieved in a less inhuman way by using other methods, the fact is that he left to his heirs a viable and strong economic and political system. Many of the Stalinist features have remained the same—others have been changed. In the following pages I shall attempt to describe the essence of Soviet society as it is today, built upon the foundations which were laid by Stalin.

III) THE KHRUSHCHEVIST SYSTEM

a) The end of the terror

The most obvious new factor by which Khrushchevism is distinguished from Stalinism is the *liquidation of the terror*. If terror was necessary in a system where the masses had to work hard without getting any corresponding material satisfaction, it could be diminished

[18] l.c. p. 335.

once the workers could begin to enjoy the fruits of their labor and could hope for increasing enjoyment. Stalin's successors were also sufficiently traumatized themselves by the crazy terror which he had exercised during his last years and which daily threatened each one of the top leaders with extinction. A psychological phenomenon, similar to that in France before the fall of Robespierre, probably existed in the Russian top leadership which led, together with the reasons first mentioned, to the decision to liquidate the terror.

All reports from Russia confirm that the system of terror has ceased to exist. The slave labor camps which were not only institutions of terror but also a source of cheap labor under Stalin were dissolved. Arbitrary arrests and punishments were abolished. The Khrushchev state might be compared with a reactionary police state of the nineteenth century as far as political freedom is concerned, perhaps not too different from the Czarist system. Yet this comparison would be misleading; not only because of the obvious differences in the economic structure of the two systems but also because of another and more complex factor. Political freedom comes up as a manifest problem only when there is considerable dissent within the fundamental structure of a given society. In the Czarist system, the majority of the population—peasants, workers, the middle class—were in opposition to the system, and the system took oppressive measures to insure its own existence. On the other hand, there is reason to assume that the Khrushchev system has succeeded in ensuring the allegiance of the majority of the Soviet population. It has done this partly by the real economic satisfactions it provides at present and the reasonable hopes for far greater improvements in the future and partly by its success in the ideological manipulation of people's minds.

From all reports it seems fairly clear that the average Russian is convinced that his system works reasonably well, looks forward to a better future, enjoys the possibilities for more education and amusement, and is mainly afraid of one thing—*war*. When he criticizes the system he criticizes details of its operation, bureaucratic stupidities, and the shoddy quality of consumer goods, but not the Soviet system as such. He certainly does not think of substituting the capitalist system for it.

No doubt under Stalin's terror the situation was quite different. The ruthless arbitrariness of the terror threatened everyone, high or low, with prison or physical extinction, not only as a result of making mistakes, but as a consequence of denunciations, intrigues, etc. But this terror has gone and things are different. The average American misjudges the Russian situation by putting himself in the role of an anti-Communist within Russia, and considering the degree to which expression of *his* opinion would be discouraged. He forgets that, apart from writers and social scientists who might be prone to criticize the system, the average Russian feels little of such an urge. Hence the problem of political freedom is by far less real for him than it appears from the American perspective. (The average Russian might feel similarly to the average American if, picturing himself as a Communist, he considered the restrictions and hazards *he* would face in the United States.) All this does not alter the fact that Khrushchev's Russia is a police state with much less freedom to dissent and to criticize the government and majority opinion than there is within the Western democracies. Furthermore, after many years of unrestricted terror, it will take years to dispell the residue of fear and intimidation created by the terror. Yet, when all is considered, the net result is that Khrushchevism marks a considerable improvement over the Stalinist era as far as political freedom is concerned.

Closely related to the disappearance of the terror system is also a change in the nature of the method of leadership in Russia. Stalin's rule was a one-man rule, without any serious consultation with collaborators and anything that in the broadest sense could be called discussion or majority rule. It is clear that such a one-man regime needed a terror-force by which the dictator could strike at any person who dared to oppose him. With the execution of Beria, the power of the terroristic state police was considerably restricted and none of the Russian leaders since Stalin's death has assumed a dictatorial position that could be compared with that of Stalin. It appears that the leader, whoever he is, has to convince the top echelon in the party of the correctness of his views, and that there is something like discussion and majority rule in the ruling committee. All events in the last few years show clearly that Khrushchev has to defend his policy against opponents, that he has to show successes in order to maintain himself on top, and that he is in some ways in a position not too different from that of a statesman in the West, whose continued political failures would lead to his political disappearance.

b) *The socio-economic structure*

The striking feature of a socialist economy is the fact that there is no private ownership in the means of production, and that all enterprises are administered by a state-appointed managerial bureaucracy. (There is, of course, private ownership of consumer goods, like

houses, furniture, automobiles, and personal accumulation of savings such as bank accounts and government bonds, just as in the United States. The difference in this respect is only that one can not own a
factory or stock in a corporation, a difference, inciden-
tally, which would be relevant only for a small part of
the population of the United States.)[19] The Soviet
leaders and their people, assuming that Marxist socialism is characterized by the ownership and management of enterprises by the state, take this to mean that
their system is socialism. Whether this claim is justified
or not will be discussed later, along with the fact that
current developments in the Soviet system are in many
respects more akin to the trends existing in twentieth-
century capitalism than they are to socialism.

Over-all planning, introduced for the first time by
Stalin's Five Year Plan in 1928, offers Soviet ideology
an additional reason to speak of their system as socialism. The over-all plan (Gosplan) is centrally made in
Moscow for the USSR after intensive deliberation over
a great amount of data. The planning determines what
is to be produced and at what rate, in contrast to the
relatively free market in the Western countries. Until
1957 the Moscow ministries for various branches of
industry were the central authorities for the respective industries under their administration. Khrushchev
abolished this centralized system, which had existed
for over twenty years, and inaugurated a process of
decentralization by replacing the ministries by regional *economic councils* (*sownarkhoz*).

These councils took over the function of the minis-

[19] In the United States 1% of all families own 4/5 of all
Industrial stocks which can be owned by individuals.
(Quoted from Robert L. Heilbroner, *The Future as History*,
Harper & Bros., New York, 1959, p. 125.)

tries in the various regions of the Soviet Union. There are somewhat over one hundred such councils within the Soviet Union. They appoint the top personnel (or confirm their appointments) in the enterprises under them, determine the production program of "their" industries (although within the framework of the general plan), are active in determining prices and production methods, and the securing of scarce materials and conduct research on the quality of products, etc. The control of the *sownarkhoz* over the many industries under its control is exercised through subdivisions, the "chief administrations," which in turn control the individual enterprises, headed by their managers.

Who are the *administrators* working in the regional councils, the chief administrations, and the individual enterprises?[20]

The majority have a college education (in fact, a greater percentage than in the United States), with the greater proportion of graduates in engineering and a smaller proportion in business administration. The vast majority of them are members of the Communist Party. (It is important for the American reader to remember that the Communist Party in Russia is, by intention, not a mass party, but represents the élite of those who want to get to the highest positions and who are willing to exert the greatest efforts; actually, only about 4 per cent of the total population are party members.) The director of a plant earns from five to ten times (including bonuses) what the worker earns, depending on the size and kind of factory.

If we compare the American situation, an American plant director would have to earn $22,000 a year to

[20] Cf. David Granick, *The Red Executive*, l.c., from which many of the following data are taken.

attain the same position in relation to the worker. The small-scale 1957 study of American firms showed that "in actual fact the top policy-making executive in firms of under 1000 employees earned an annual average of $28,000 in salary and bonus."[21]

These figures are difficult to compare since on the one hand prices for consumer goods are relatively much higher in the Soviet Union than in the United States, while on the other hand rents are much lower in the Soviet Union and fringe benefits are higher than in the United States. Thus, the income differential between managers and workers is not too different in the Soviet Union from what it is in the United States.

What is particularly important is the role of bonuses, which reach 50 to 100 per cent of the manager's salary and which constitute the most important incentive for optimal production. (Often this system emphasizes quantity rather than quality—hence leading to the production of inferior consumer goods.) Thus, the managers represent a social group that in income, consumption, and authority, is as different from the workers as in any capitalist country of the West. In fact, judging from many reports, rigidities in class stratification, status-differential, etc., are greater than in the United States.

There is one more important characteristic of the managerial group. Granick reports that Soviet data show that, as early as the 1930s, a great deal of social stability had developed. "Statistics on this subject," writes Granick, "unfortunately end in the 1930s. Moreover, the data as to the occupation of parents is broken down into only a threefold classification: worker, farmer, and white-collar. Still, even this data is rea-

[21] Cf. D. Granick, l.c. pp. 41–42.

sonably strong. It shows that the son of a white collar employee, professional or business owner, had eight times as good a chance of reaching top management rank in the United States [in 1952] as did the sons of manual workers and farmers, and that he had *six times as good a chance in the Soviet Union* [1936]."[22]

As far as the situation today is concerned, one can only guess. But Granick sounds convincing when he says that the tendency against social mobility "has probably increased in present-day Russia simply because of the lesser amount of hostility toward the children of white collar parents."[23] This class stratification exists in spite of the fact that education in the Soviet Union is absolutely free and most of the better students receive stipends besides. This apparent contradiction is probably explained to some extent by the fact that many young Soviet people may not be able to go on to college because their families need their earnings.[24] Considering the very high scholastic standards of Russian higher education, it would also appear likely that the cultural atmosphere of a managerial family provides a better preparation in this respect than that of a worker's or peasant's family.

The surprising fact—surprising for those who believe in the socialist character of the Soviet system—is, as Berliner reports, that to be a "worker" is "something devoutly to be shunned by most young people who have reached the high school level."[25] This attitude toward being a worker is, of course, not expressed in the offi-

[22] D. Granick, l.c. p. 54 (my italics, E.F.).

[23] D. Granick, l.c. p. 56.

[24] Cf. Joseph S. Berliner, Managerial Incentives and Decision Making, *Congr. Committee Papers,* p. 352.

[25] l.c. p. 350.

cial ideology, which extolls the workers as being the true masters of Soviet society, and the myth of great social mobility continues to exist in the Soviet Union.

Is it correct, then, to speak of a managerial *class* in the Soviet Union? If one uses Marx's concept, the term "class" could not very well be applied, since in Marxist thought this refers to a social group with reference to its relation to the means of production; that is, whether the group owns capital or its tools (artisans), or is made up of propertyless workers. Naturally in a country where the state owns all the means of production there is no managerial "class" in this sense, nor any other for that matter, and, if one uses the term "class" in a strict Marxist sense, one can claim that the Soviet Union is a classless society.

In reality, however, this is not so. Marx did not foresee that in the development of capitalist society there would be a vast group of managers who, while not owning the means of production, exercise control over them, and who have in common a high income and high social status.[26] Hence Marx never transcended his concept of class beyond that of *ownership of the means of production* to that of *control* of the means of production and of the "human material" employed in the process of production, distribution, and consumption.

In terms of *control*, the Soviet Union is a society with rigid class distinctions. Aside from the managerial bureaucracy, there are the political bureaucracy of the Communist Party and the military bureaucracy. All

[26] Cf. A. A. Berle, Jr. and C. Means, *The Modern Corporation and Private Property*, The Macmillan Company, New York, 1948 and Joseph A. Schumpeter, *Capitalism, Socialism and Democracy*, third edition, Harper & Bros., New York, 1958.

three share control, prestige, and income. It is important to note that they largely overlap. Not only are most managers and top officers members of the party, but also they often "change hats," that is, work for a time as managers, and then again as party officials.[27] On the fringes of the three bureaucracies are the scientists, other intellectuals and artists, who are highly rewarded although they do not share in the power of the three main groups.

The foregoing considerations make one point clear. The Soviet Union, in the process of developing into a highly industrialized system, has not only produced new factories and machines but also new classes, which direct and administer production. These classes have acquired interests of their own, which are quite different from those of the revolutionaries who took over in 1917. They are interested in material comforts, in security, and in education and social advancement for their children, in short, in the very same aims as the corresponding classes in capitalist countries.

The continued existence of the *myth* of equality, however, does not mean that the *fact* of the rise of a Soviet hierarchy is disputed in Russia. Stalin quite overtly—and of course always quoting the proper passages from Marx and Lenin out of context—as early as 1925 warned the Fourteenth Congress: "We must not play with the phrase about equality. This is playing with fire."[28] As Deutscher puts it: Stalin, in later years, spoke "against the 'levellers' with a rancour and venom which suggested that in doing so he defended the most sensitive and vulnerable facet of his policy.

[27] In 1936, 98% of all factory directors in heavy industry were Party members. (Quoted from Granick, l.c. p. 309.)
[28] Quoted by I. Deutscher, *Stalin*, l.c. p. 339.

It was so sensitive because the highly paid and privileged managerial groups came to be the props of Stalin's regime."[29] In fact, the Soviet Union copes with the same problem as the capitalist countries do —namely how to reconcile the ideology of an open, mobile society with the need for a hierarchically organized bureaucracy and how to give prestige and moral justification to those on top. The Soviet solution is not too different from our own; both principles are emphasized, and the individual is supposed not to stumble over the contradiction.

The growth of Soviet industry not only produced a new class of managers, but also a growing class of manual workers. In 1928, 76.5 per cent of the Russian population were dependent on agricultural occupations, as against 23.5 per cent on nonagricultural occupations; by 1958 the ratio was 52 per cent to 48 per cent respectively.[30] But the development of industry requires more than an ever larger number of industrial workers. It also requires increasing productivity of the labor force. How serious this necessity is for the Soviet Union is illustrated by the fact that in the machine-building industry, according to the official journal of the Gosplan, United States labor productivity is 2.8 to 3 times higher than it is in the Soviet Union.[31] Aside from the higher level of technology, one of the decisive factors in labor productivity is the character of the workers themselves. In order to further the development of a more independent and responsible charac-

[29] l.c. p. 339.

[30] Warren W. Eason, The Labor Force, *Congr. Committee Papers*, p. 75.

[31] Figures quoted from Leon Herman, "The Labor Force: Who Does What?" *Saturday Review*, January 21, 1961, p. 34 ff.

ter, not only have punitive policies been replaced, (absenteeism, for instance, which under Stalin was a criminal offense, is now a disciplinary matter to be dealt with by management), but "Soviet labor policy has moved in many respects to encourage the positive manifestations of application and effectiveness on the job," [in the area of wage policy and even in the worker's greater role in the day-to-day decision-making of the enterprise] "without, however, fundamentally usurping the prerogatives of management."[32]

The roles of education, material satisfaction, and incentives are generally recognized by the Soviet hierarchy as being of basic importance, and the state is trying its best to improve these factors and thus to increase labor productivity. This development will undoubtedly lead to the very thing it has led to in the Western countries. The workers not only work better, they are also more satisfied and more loyal to the system: in the one case "capitalism," in the other "communism."

While the gap between the situations of the workers in both systems is narrowing, there is one difference that shows no signs of being erased, a political and psychological rather than an economic one—the absence of independent trade unions in the Soviet Union. The "company union" character of their unions is, of course, denied by Soviet ideology. The reasoning is that a workers' state, in which the workers themselves "own" the means of production, does not need the type of unions the workers need under capitalism. But this reasoning is mainly, of course, ideological. The crucial point is that the domination of the unions by party and state in the Soviet Union stifles the spirit of in-

[32] W. W. Eason, l.c. p. 92.

dependence and freedom and thus tends to strengthen the authoritarian character of the whole Soviet system.

c) Education and morals

The *educational system* of the Soviet Union serves, like that of any other country, to prepare the individual for the function he is to assume in society. The first task is to inculcate those attitudes and values that are dominant in Soviet society. The values impressed on Soviet youth and citizens correspond to the dominant Western morality, although heavily accented on the conservative side. "Care, responsibility, love, patriotism, diligence, honesty, industriousness, the injunction against transgressing the happiness of one's fellowman, consideration for the common interest—there is nothing in this catalogue of values that could not be included in the ethics of the Western tradition."[33]

Respect for property is emphasized as respect for socialist property, submission to authority as acceptance of national or international solidarity. As far as sexual morality is concerned, Soviet morality is conservative and puritanical. The family is praised as a center of social stability, and any kind of sexual promiscuity is sternly discouraged. Since the betrayal of the party or the Soviet system is about the worst imaginable crime in Soviet morality, the following statement gives an idea of this Soviet puritanism. *Komsomolskaya Pravda* (April 1959) asked in reporting a case of marital betrayal: "How many steps are there from this to treason in the broader sense . . . ?"[34] Communism is

[33] H. Marcuse, l.c. p. 232. Cf. his excellent chapter on ethics, pp. 195–267.

[34] Quoted from Erich Goldhagen, The Glorious Future, Realities and Chimeras, *Problems of Communism*, November–December 1960, pp. 10–18.

described as a system of "consistent monogamy" and as being opposed in principle to liaisons born of "dissoluteness and flightiness."[35] Aside from the central goal of Soviet education, dutiful subordination of the individual to the demands of Soviet society and its representatives, the other aim is that of creating the proper spirit of a competitive work morality. The following statement, adopted by the Central Committee of the Komsomol shows how even the family is to serve the needs for proper labor training. "Families in which a genuine mutual concern about cultural growth is evident and domestic responsibilities are properly shared by all members of the family should be held up as examples. It is necessary to encourage the participation of children, adolescents, and young men and women in the performance of domestic chores and to appreciate this as an important and integral part of labor training."[36]

Leisure, just as family life, should serve labor training. It should not serve "idle pleasure," but it should make man better fitted for his social integration and for better work habits. This is very succinctly expressed in the following statement: "With the expansion of free time under socialism, each working person receives greater opportunity to raise his cultural level, to perfect his knowledge; he can better fulfill his social obligations and raise his children, better organize his rest, participate in sports, and so on. All this is necessary for the all-sided development of a human being. Simultaneously, free time . . . serves a powerful factor in

[35] A. Kharchew, *Kommunist,* Nov. 7, 1960, p. 63, quoted from E. Goldhagen, l.c. p. 17.

[36] *Komsomolskaya Pravda,* August 5, 1960, p. 3, quoted from Goldhagen, l.c. p. 17.

raising labor productivity. It was in this sense that Marx called free time the greatest productive force exerting an influence in turn on the productive force of labor. Thus free time and working time are interconnected and interdependent."[37] (It should be noted in passing that this reference to Marx is a cynical falsification; Marx speaks of free time precisely as the true realm of freedom, which begins when work ends, and in which man can unfold his own powers as an aim in itself, and not as a means for the end of production.) How far a Soviet leader like Khrushchev has even ideologically moved away from the Marxist concept of socialism becomes very clear from a conversation between President Sukarno and Khrushchev. Sukarno stated, in a simple yet essentially correct way, the traditional socialist concept: "Indonesian socialism . . . aims at a good life for all without exploitation." Khrushchev: "No, no, no. Socialism should mean that every minute is calculated, a life built on calculation." Sukarno: "That is the life of a robot."[38] He might have added: and your definition of socialism is actually the definition of the capitalist principle.

In some respects, as Marcuse has pointed out, Soviet morality is similar to Calvinist work morale: they both *reflect the need for the incorporation of large masses of 'backward' people into a new social system, the need for the creation of a well-trained, disciplined labor force, capable of vesting the perpetual routine of the working day with ethical sanction, producing ever more rationally, ever-increasing amounts of goods,

[37] G. Prudenski, in *Kommunist,* Nov. 16, 1960, quoted from Goldhagen, l.c. p. 18.

[38] *The New York Times,* March 2, 1960, quoted from E. Goldhagen, l.c. p. 10.

while the rational use of these goods for the individual's needs is ever more delayed by the circumstances."[39] At the same time, however, the Soviet Union makes use of the most modern technology, machinery and production methods, and hence has to combine the need for intelligent imagination, individual initiative and responsibility, with the needs of an old-fashioned, traditional labor discipline. The Soviet system in its organization methods as well as in its psychological aims, combines (or "telescopes," as Marcuse aptly says) older with very new phases, and it is precisely this telescoping which makes the understanding of it so difficult for the Western observer—not to speak of the added difficulty that this system is expressed in ideological terms of Marxist humanism and eighteenth-century enlightenment philosophy.

While Soviet ideology pays lip service to Marx's ideal of the "all-rounded personality" who is not shackled to one and the same occupation all his life, Soviet education places all the emphasis on *Training*—the training of "specialists on the basis of a close co-operation between studies and production" and calls for "strengthening [of] the ties of the country's scientific establishment with production, with the concrete demands of the national economy."[40]

Soviet culture is centered around intellectual development, while it neglects the development of the affective side of man. This latter fact finds its expression in the low standards of Soviet literature, painting,

[39] H. Marcuse, l.c. p. 239. Cf. also the analysis of the social function of Calvinistic ethics in E. Fromm, *Escape from Freedom*, Rinehart & Co., New York, 1941.

[40] Resolution adopted by the 20th congress of the Communist Party of the Soviet Union, quoted from H. Marcuse, l.c. p. 183.

architecture and moving pictures. In the name of "socialist realism" a low level of Victorian bourgeois taste is cultivated, and this in a country that, especially in literature and films, was once among the most creative in the world. While in certain traditional arts like the ballet and the performing of music the Russian people show still the same gifts they had for many generations, the arts that are related to ideology and that influence people's minds, especially films and literature, show nothing of this creativeness. They breathe the spirit of extreme utilitarianism, are cheap exhortations to work, discipline, patriotism, etc. The absence of any authentic human feeling, love, sadness, or doubt, betrays a degree of alienation that is hardly surpassed anywhere else in the world. In these films and novels, men and women have been transformed into things, useful for production, and alienated from themselves and one another. (Of course it remains to be seen whether the change from Stalinism to Khrushchevism will eventually lead to a marked improvement in the artistic standard of Soviet culture, and that means in the degree of alienation existing now; such a development seems possible only if very fundamental changes were to take place in the social system of the Soviet Union.)

These facts seem perhaps to be contradicted by another set of facts, namely the large amount of "good" literature (Dostoevski, Tolstoi, Balzac, etc.), which is published and presumably read in the Soviet Union. A number of authors who believe that the Khrushchev system might be the basis from which a genuine humanist socialism will develop have often quoted this aspect of Soviet book-publishing as an argument for their hopes. If people are imbued with this kind of literature to the degree that they are in the Soviet Union, so they argue, their human development will be molded by the spirit of this literature. I do not find this argument very convincing. It is only logical that a population that is being driven into a state of ever-increasing alienation is starved for genuine human experience, as it is represented in "good" literature. But the very fact that the novels by Dostoevski, Balzac, or Jack London take place in foreign countries or in cultures entirely different from Soviet reality makes them serve as high-class escape literature; this literature satisfies the unquenchable thirst for authentic human experience which remains unsatisfied in the contemporary Soviet practice, and yet, being completely disconnected from this practice, also does not endanger it.

If we want to look for a parallel phenomenon in the Western culture one has only to remember that the Bible is still the most widely sold and presumably the most widely read book in the West, and yet that this same book fails to have any marked influence on the real experience of modern man, either on his feelings or on his actions. In short, the Bible has become escape literature, needed to save the individual from facing the abyss of emptiness that his mode of life opens up before him, yet without much effect because no connection is made between the Bible and his real life.

CHAPTER THREE

Is world domination the aim of the Soviet Union?

United States policy and public opinion are based on the premises that the Soviet Union is a) a socialist state, and b) a revolutionary and/or imperialist system with the aim of world conquest. Each of these premises deserves minute examination. At the same time attention must be paid to the connection between the internal social structure of the Soviet Union and its revolutionary and/or imperialist trends for world domination.

1) IS THE SOVIET UNION A SOCIALIST SYSTEM?

According to the leaders of the Soviet Union, the "Union of Socialist Soviet Republics" is socialist not only in name but in fact. Already in 1936 Stalin proclaimed "the complete victory of the socialist system in all spheres of the national economy,"[1] and at the present time Soviet ideology claims that the Soviet Union is moving rapidly toward the realization of communism. (Characterized by Marx's famous statement: "From each according to his capacities, to each according to his needs.")[2]

[1] J. Stalin, *Problems of Leninism,* Foreign Languages Publishing House, Moscow, 1947 edition, p. 548.

[2] K. Marx, *Critique of the Gotha Programme.*

The question of the socialist character of the Soviet Union can be decided only by making a comparison between Marx's vision of socialism and the reality of the Soviet system. What rationale do the Soviet leaders from Stalin to Khrushchev have for calling their system socialism? They make this claim essentially on the basis of their definition of Marxist socialism, in which two factors are considered decisive for a socialist society: the "socialization of the means of production" and a planned economy. But Socialism in the sense of Marx or, for that matter, in the sense of Owen, Hess, Fourier, Proudhon, etc., can not be defined in this way.

What was the essence of Marx's thought and of Marxist socialism? It is bewildering how Marx's theory is falsified and vilified not only by the ignorant, but also by many who should and could know better. As Robert L. Heilbroner has put it so well: our public newspapers and books "obscure the fact that the literature of socialist protest is one of the most moving and morally searching of all chronicles of human hope and despair. To dismiss the literature unread, to vilify it without the faintest conception of what it represents, is not only shocking but dangerously stupid."[3]

The very beginning of an understanding of Marx is blocked by one of the most widespread and completely erroneous clichés, that of Marx's "materialism."[4] This

[3] Robert L. Heilbroner, *The Future as History,* Harper & Bros., New York, 1959, pp. 113–14.

[4] I have pointed out this fallacy in an article "Uber Aufgabe und Methode einer analytischen Sozialpsychologie" (On the Method and Aim of Analytic Social Psychology) Ztschr. für Sozialforschung, C. L. Hirschfeld, Leipzig, 1932, Vol. I. Schumpeter has made the same point in *Capitalism, Socialism and Democracy,* Harper & Bros., New York, 1947.

materialism is supposed to mean that the main motivation in man is his wish for material gain, as against spiritual, moral or religious values. While it is rather paradoxical that those who attack Marx for this alleged materialism defend capitalism against socialism with the claim that only a monetary incentive can be a sufficiently strong motivation for man to give his best, the fact is that Marx's theory is precisely the opposite of this alleged materialism. His main criticism of capitalism was that it is a system that puts a premium on selfish and materialistic motivations, and his concept of socialism was that of a society that favors men who *are* much instead of *having* much. Marx's historical materialism never speaks of the economic factor as a *psychological* motivation, but as a socio-economic *condition* that leads to a certain practice of life and thus shapes man's character. His difference with Hegel's idealism (idealism and materialism are philosophical terms and have nothing to do with ideal versus materialistic motivation, as any high school student should know), lies in the fact that ". . . we do not set out from what men imagine, conceive, nor from men as narrated, thought of, or imagined, conceived, in order to arrive at men in the flesh. *We set out from real, active men and on the basis of their real life process* we demonstrate the development of the ideological reflexes and echoes of the life process."[5] Or, as he put it elsewhere: "As individuals express their life, so they are. What they are, therefore, coincides with their production. Both with *what* they produce and with *how* they produce. The nature of individuals thus depends on the material conditions determining their produc-

[5] K. Marx and F. Engels, *Die Heilige Familie* (*The Holy Family*), 1845 (my translation, E.F.).

tion."[6] Marx's discovery was that the practice of life, as it is determined by the economic systems, determines the feeling and thinking of the people involved. According to this view, a certain system may be conducive to the development of materialistic strivings; another system may lead to the preponderance of ascetic tendencies.[7]

The main concern of Marx was, as was Hegel's, the full development of man's potentialities, the subject, as Hegel put it, "translating itself from the night of possibility into the day of actuality." Man, so Marx taught, develops his potentialities in the process of history. He *ought* to be that which he *could* be, yet which he not yet is. In modern industrial society, man, according to Marx, has reached the peak of *alienation*. In the act of production, the relationship of the worker to his own activity is experienced as something "not belonging to him." While man thus becomes alienated from himself, the product of labor becomes "an alien object which dominates him. The laborer exists for the process of production, and not the process of production for the laborer."[8] Not only do the things that man produces become his rulers, so do the social and political circumstances which he creates. "This consolidation of what we ourselves produce which turns into an objective

[6] K. Marx, F. Engels, *The German Ideology*, International Publ. Inc., New York, 1939, p. 7.

[7] In the concept of the "social character" I have tried to analyze the connection between the socio-economic structure of a society and the prevalent emotional and intellectual attitudes (cf. *Escape from Freedom*, Rinehart & Co. Inc., New York, 1941, and my older paper, "Uber Aufgabe und Methode einer analytischen Sozialpsychologie").

[8] Karl Marx, *Capital*, Charles H. Kerr, Chicago, 1906, Vol. I, p. 536.

power above us, growing out of our control, thwarting our expectations, bringing to naught our calculations, is one of the chief factors in historical development up to now."[9] That man, the fully developed, productive man be the *subject* and not the *object* of history, that man cease to be "a crippled monstrosity and becomes a fully developed human being" is, according to Marx, the aim of socialism.

Man's aim, in Marx's concept, is *independence and freedom.* "A being," he says, "does not regard himself as independent unless he is his own master and he is only his own master when he owes his existence to himself. A man who lives by the favor of another considers himself a dependent being."[10] As Marx put it, man is independent only if he "appropriates his manifold being in an all-inclusive way, and thus as a whole man. All his *human* relations to the world—seeing, hearing, smelling, tasting, touching, thinking, observing, feeling, desiring, acting, loving—in short, all the organs of his individuality . . . are . . . the appropriation of human reality . . . Private Property has made us so stupid and partial that an object is only *ours* when we have it, when it exists for us as capital or when it is directly eaten, drunk, worn, inhabited, etc., in short, *utilized* in some way; . . . Thus *all* the physical and intellectual senses have been replaced by the simple alienation of *all* these senses; the sense of *having.* The human being

[9] German Ideology, l.c. p. 23. There could hardly be a more drastic example for this power of things over men than the nuclear weapons, which man created, and yet which now seem to control him.

[10] *Marx's Concept of Man*, E. Fromm, with a translation from Marx's Economic and Philosophical Manuscripts of 1844 by T. B. Bottomore, Frederick Ungar Publishing Co., 1961, p. 138.

had to be reduced to this absolute poverty in order to be able to give birth to all his inner wealth."[11]

Marx's idea of the full self-realization of man implies that this self-realization can occur only in man's relatedness to the world, to nature, to his fellow man and in the relationship of men to women. That socialism was, for Marx, as Paul Tillich has put it "a resistance movement against the destruction of love in social reality,"[12] becomes very evident from the following passage: "Let us assume man and his relation to the world to be a human one. Then love can only be exchanged for love, trust for trust, etc. If you wish to influence other people, you must be a person who really has a stimulating and encouraging effect upon others. Every one of your relations to man and to nature must be a *specific expression* corresponding to the object of your will, of your *real individual* life. If you love without evoking love in return, i.e. if you are not able by the manifestation of yourself as a loving person, to make yourself *a beloved person*, then your love is impotent, a misfortune."[13]

The productive, free, independent, loving individual —this was Marx's vision of man. He was not concerned with maximum production and consumption, although he was in favor of making possible for everybody the attainment of an economic level that is the basis of a humanly dignified life. He was also not primarily concerned with the equalization of income, although he would have been opposed to such inequality as pre-

[11] l.c. pp. 131–32.
[12] Protestantische Vision (Protestant Vision) Ring Verlag, Stuttgart, 1952, p. 6. (My translation E.F.)
[13] l.c. p. 168.

vents men from sharing the same basic experiences of life. Marx's central concern was with the liberation of man from the kind of work which destroys his individuality, transforms him into a thing, and enslaves him to the things of his own creation.

Marx's concepts are rooted in Prophetic Messianism, in Renaissance individualism, and in enlightenment humanism. The philosophy underlying his concepts is that of the active, productive, related individual, a philosophy of which the names of Spinoza, Goethe and Hegel are most representative.

That Marx's idea was deformed and corrupted into its very opposite, both by the Communists and by the capitalist opponents of socialism, is a remarkable—though by no means unique—example of man's capacity for distortion and irrationality. However, in order to understand whether the Soviet Union and China represent Marxist socialism, and what might be expected from truly socialist societies, it is important that we have an idea of what Marxism means.

That Marx himself would not have considered the Soviet Union or China a socialist state follows from the following statement: "This [vulgar] communism,[14] which negates the *personality* of man in every sphere, is only the logical expression of private property, which *is* this negation. Universal *envy* setting itself up as a power is only a camouflaged form of cupidity which re-establishes itself and satisfies itself in a different way. The thoughts of every individual private property are *at least* directed against any *wealthier* private property, in the form of envy and the desire to reduce

[14] Marx refers here to certain eccentric Communist thinkers of his time, who claimed that communism meant a commune whose members should have everything in common.

everything to a common level; so that this envy and leveling in fact constitute the essence of competition. Crude communism is only the culmination of such envy and leveling-down on the basis of a *preconceived* minimum. How little this abolition of private property represents a genuine appropriation is shown by the abstract negation of the whole world of culture and civilization, and the regression to the *unnatural* simplicity of the poor and wantless individual who has not only not surpassed private property but has not yet even attained to it. The community is only a community of *work* and of *equality of wages* paid out by the communal capital, by the *community* as universal capitalist. The two sides of the relation are raised to a *supposed* universality; *labor* as a condition in which everyone is placed, and *capital* as the acknowledged universality and power of the community."[15, 16]

It was *not* Marx who believed in the negation of personality, and that socialism meant the leveling of all men. His errors are of a different kind, and have nothing to do with the underestimation of individuality. He underestimated the complexity and strength of man's irrational passions and his readiness to accept systems that could relieve him of the responsibility and burden of freedom. He underestimated the resilience

[15] l.c., p. 125.

[16] It should be added here that the Russian writers on Marxism have claimed that certain ideas which are contained in these early writings were abandoned by the later Marx. While he changed his terminology somewhat, there is no doubt that the essential humanist ideas of the young Marx underlie his thinking throughout his life, to the last pages of the Capital. A detailed discussion of the continuity of Marx's thought is to be found in "Marx's Concept of Man."

of capitalism and the many new forms into which this system could evolve and thus avoid the necessarily catastrophic results, as assumed by Marx, of its inner contradictions. Another error of Marx was that he could not free himself sufficiently from the decisive importance nineteenth-century thought gave to legal property. Legal ownership then was identical with management and social control. Hence Marx concluded that if legal ownership were taken away from the private capitalist and vested in society the workers would direct their own affairs. Little did he see that a change in ownership may only be a change in control, from the owners to a bureaucracy acting in the name of the stockholders or of the state, and that this change may have little or no effect on the real situation of the workers within the system of production.

Generations later nationalized industries in England, France, and Russia have shown this very clearly. Theoretically the Guild socialists in England and, both theoretically and practically, the Yugoslav Communists, have recognized the ambiguous character of state ownership, and have built a system based on the ownership *and* control of factories by the workers, rather than by the state and its bureaucracy.

As I pointed out before, with the increasing development of capitalism, not only economically but psychologically, the spiritual, humanistic aims of socialism were replaced by those of the victorious capitalist system—the aims of maximal economic efficiency, maximal production and consumption. This misinterpretation of socialism as a purely economic movement, along with an acceptance of the nationalization of the means of production as an aim in itself, occurred both in the right and left wings of the socialist movement. The primary aim of the reformist leaders of the socialist movement in Europe was the elevation of the economic status of the worker *within* the capitalist system. Their most radical measure in this effort was the nationalization of certain big industries. Only recently has it been realized that the nationalization of an enterprise is in itself not the realization of socialism, and that to be managed by a publicly appointed bureaucracy is not basically different for the worker from being managed by a privately appointed bureaucracy. The leaders of the Soviet Union evaluate socialism also by the standards of capitalism, and their principal claim for the Soviet system is that "socialism" can produce more effectively and abundantly than "capitalism."

Both wings of socialism forget that Marx aimed at a humanly different society, not only at a more prosperous one. His concept of socialism, despite changes in the development of his own thinking, was principally that of an unalienated society in which every citizen would be an active and responsible member of the community, participating in the control of all social and economic arrangements and not, as in the Soviet practice, a "number," fed with ideologies and controlled by a small bureaucratic minority. For Marx, socialism was the control of society from below, by its members; not from above, by a bureaucracy. The Soviet Union may be called state capitalism, or anything else; one claim this managerial, bureaucratic system can not make is that of being "socialism" in Marx's sense. No better answer can be given to this claim than Schumpeter's statement that there is "between the true meaning of Marx's message and Bolshevist practice and ideology at least as great a gulf as there was between the religion of humble Gallileans and the practice and ideology of the princes of the Church or the warlords of the Middle Ages."[17]

While the Soviet system has borrowed the concept of the nationalization of the means of production and of over-all planning from Marxist socialism, it nonetheless shares many features with contemporary capitalism.

The *development of twentieth-century capitalism* has led to an ever-growing centralization in industrial production. The big corporations are becoming increasingly the center of production in the steel, automobile, and chemical industries, in oil, food, banking, movies, and television. Only in certain branches of production, like the clothing industry, do we still find the nineteenth-century picture of a great number of small and highly competitive enterprises. Today's big enterprises are directed by vast and hierarchically structured bureaucracies, which administer the enterprise according to the principles of profit maximization, yet are relatively independent of the millions of stockholders who are the legal owners. The same centralization has taken place in government, in the armed forces, and even in scientific research.

While "private enterprise" decries ideologically all socialist tendencies, it is eager to accept large direct and indirect grants by the state. The same development has led to important changes with regard to free competition and the free market. The free market and free competition in the nineteenth-century sense are phenomena of the past.

[17] Joseph A. Schumpeter, *Capitalism, Socialism and Democracy,* Harper & Bros., New York, third edition, 1950, p. 3.

Even though the Western systems retain some measure of competition, overt and hidden price agreements between the big corporations, state grants, etc., have (in spite of anti-monopoly laws in the United States) greatly restricted competition and the function of the free market. Assuming, for a moment, that the tendency toward centralization develops further, and that there will eventually be only one big corporation producing, respectively, automobiles, steel, films, etc., the picture of "capitalist" economy would not be so drastically different from the Russian socialist economy. There is of course an increasing element of state planning in Western capitalism, not only through massive state intervention, but also in the sense that the Atomic Energy Commission is the largest industrial enterprise in the United States, and that the armament industry, although in private hands, produces a great mass of weapons according to plans made by the state. This, however, does not imply that there is over-all planning in the United States beyond arms production, or even a plan for the transition from an armament to a peace economy.

The mode of production in contemporary capitalism is that of large conglomerations of workers and clerks who work under the orders of the managerial bureaucracies. They are part of a vast production machine which, in order to run at all, must run smoothly, without friction, without interruption. The individual worker or clerk becomes a cog in this machine; his functions and activities are determined by the whole structure of the organization in which he works. In the large enterprises, legal ownership of the means of production has become separated from its management, and has lost importance. The managers do not have the qualities of the old owners—individual initiative, daring, risk-taking—but the qualities of the bureaucrat—lack of individuality and imagination, impersonality, caution. They administer *things and persons,* and relate to persons as to things. The giant corporations, which control the economic—and to a large degree the political—destiny of the country, constitute the very opposite of the democratic process; they represent power without control by those whom they rule.

Aside from the industrial bureaucracy, the vast majority of the population is administered by still other bureaucracies. First, there is the governmental bureaucracy, (including that of the armed forces) which influences and directs the lives of many millions in one form or another. More and more, the industrial, military and governmental bureaucracies are becoming intertwined, both in their activities and, increasingly, in their personnel. With the development of ever greater enterprises, unions also have developed into big bureaucratic machines in which the individual member has very little to say. Many union chiefs are managerial bureaucrats, just as the industrial chiefs are.

All these bureaucracies have little authentic vision; and, due to the very nature of bureaucratic administration, this has to be so. They function rather like electronic computers, into which all the data have been fed and which—according to certain principles—make the "decisions." When man is transformed into a thing and managed like a thing, his managers themselves become things; and things have no will, no vision, no plan.[18]

With the bureaucratic management of people, the

[18] An "old-fashioned" capitalist, J. Paul Getty, recently wrote as follows on this point: "In my estimation, the mania for conformity can do the Free World's cause more harm than a dozen Nikita Khrushchevs." ("Money and Conformity," *Playboy,* February 1960, p. 135.)

democratic process becomes transformed into a ritual. Whether it is a stockholders meeting, or a political election, or a union meeting, the individual has lost almost all power to participate actively in the making of decisions. Especially in the political sphere, elections become more and more reduced to plebiscites in which the voter can express preference for one of two slates of professional politicians. The best that can be said for this is that he is governed with his consent. But the means used to bring about this consent are those of suggestion and manipulation and, with all that, the most fundamental decisions—those of foreign policy which involve peace and war—are made by small groups, which the average citizen hardly even knows of.

Not only is the individual managed and manipulated in the sphere of production, but also in the sphere of consumption, which allegedly is the one in which he can express his free choice. Whether it is the consumption of food, clothing, liquor, cigarettes, or of films and television programs, a powerful suggestion apparatus is employed for two purposes: first, to increase constantly the appetite for new commodities, and second, to direct these appetites into the channels most profitable for industry. The very size of the capital investment in the consumer goods industry and the competition between a few giant enterprises makes it necessary not to leave consumption to chance, nor to leave the consumer a free choice of whether he wants to buy more and what he wants to buy. His appetites have to be constantly whetted; his tastes have to be manipulated, managed, and made predictable. Man is transformed into the "consumer," the eternal suckling, whose one wish is to consume more and "better" things.

The Soviet Union serves as a warning to Western industrialism of where we will arrive if we continue in our present direction. In the West we have developed a managerial industrialism, with the concomitant "organization man"; Russia, having jumped over the intermediate stage in which we in the West still find ourselves, has carried this development to its logical end —under the names of Marxism and socialism. Nationalization (the abolition of private property in the means of production) is not an essential distinction between "socialism" and "capitalism." It is merely a technical device for more efficient production and planning. The Soviet system is an efficient, completely centralized system, ruled by an industrial, political and military bureaucracy; it is the completed "managerial revolution," rather than a socialist revolution. The Soviet system is not the opposite of the capitalist system, but rather the image into which capitalism will develop unless we return to the principles of the Western tradition of humanism and individualism.

If concentrated ownership of property, bureaucratic management of the process of production, and manipulated consumption are essential elements of twentieth-century capitalism, the difference from Soviet communism seems to be one of degree rather than of quality. If capitalism, as Keynes said, can survive only with a considerable degree of socialization, it may be said with equal justification that Soviet communism has survived by incorporating a considerable amount of capitalism. In fact, the Soviet system and the Western system are both confronted with the same problems of industrialization and economic growth in a highly developed, centralized managerial society.[19] They both

[19] Cf. W. W. Eason's paper, *Congr. Committee Papers,* l.c. p. 93 and *Industrialism and Industrial Man,* by C. Kerr, J. T. Dunlop, F. Harbison, and C. A. Myers, Harvard University Press, Cambridge, 1960.

use the methods of a managerial, bureaucratically ruled mass society characterized by an increasing degree of human alienation, adaptation to the group, and a prevalence of material over spiritual interests; they both produce the organization man who is ruled by the bureaucracies and the machines and yet believes himself to be following the lofty aim of humanistic ideals.

The similarities between the Soviet system and "capitalism" were strikingly demonstrated in the presentation of the class stratification and the educational goals of the Soviet Union, a comparison which shows that in many respects the Soviet system resembles the capitalist system of the nineteenth century while in some others it is more modern and "advanced" than that of the West. These similarities become even clearer if we consider one factor that, in Western opinion, is the cornerstone of capitalism: *monetary incentives*. What are the facts about incentives in Soviet Russia?

As far as the *workers* in Russia are concerned the incentive is cash. The cash incentive operates in two ways. First, is the fact that wages are for the most part based on the piece-work principle. Wages "are fixed for the required output planned for the specific job. As the worker exceeds his quota, the incentive system sets up a rising scale to compensate him for increased production. For the laborer who raises his output from 1 to 10 per cent, the commensurate increase in the piece rate is 100 per cent."[20] If he consistently doubles his quota his monthly pay will be almost double his regular wage. The second cash incentive for the worker is bonuses, which are paid out of the profit of the enter-

[20] Benjamin A. Javits, A Comparison of Incentives in the Economic System of the United States and Soviet Russia, *Congr. Committee Papers*, p. 343.

prise. "In many cases the bonus will make up the larger amount of a Russian worker's annual wages."[21]

As far as Soviet *managers* are concerned, the chief incentive is that of the bonus paid for the overfulfillment of targets. "The amount of income earned in the form of bonuses is substantial. In 1947 . . . the managerial personnel of the iron and steel industry earned bonuses averaging 51.4 per cent of their basic income. In the food industry at the low end, the percentage was 21 per cent. Since these are averages, many individual managers earned considerably more than this. Bonuses of this magnitude must be a potent incentive indeed."[22] Also the status symbol and the expense account have become, according to Javits, an important incentive for the Soviet manager. Summing up, Berliner states that "private gain has for the last 25 years been the keystone of the management incentive system" and "we are safe in saying that for the next several decades at least, private gain will be the central economic incentive in both [the American and the Russian] systems."[23]

For the *peasants* too, cash is one of the main economic incentives. "There is one incentive," Javits points out, "that is paradoxical insofar as it shows a relaxation of state incentive on the one hand by the Soviet, and a continued experimentation on the other hand by the United States. It refers to the highly pub-

[21] Benjamin A. Javits, l.c. p. 343.

[22] Joseph S. Berliner, Managerial Incentives and Decision Making: A Comparison between the United States and the Soviet Union, *Congr. Committee Papers*, p. 356, cf. the whole paper for the question of managerial incentives; also the same author's *Factory and Manager in the U.S.S.R.*, Harvard University Press, Cambridge, 1957.

[23] l.c. p. 355.

licized incentive to agriculture offered by the United States at its expense for the private gain of the farmer. . . . In the Soviet Union . . . after having sold the required crop to the government, the members of the collectives are permitted to market the excess to the public on a supply-and-demand basis. This area of Soviet economy is about the only one in which a free market can be found."[24]

Russia is still a reactionary welfare state; we are still a liberal welfare state. But it is to be assumed that things in the Soviet Union will slowly change. Clearly, the more the Soviet Union can satisfy the material needs of her population, the less will she need the methods of the police state. The Soviet system will shift to the same means that are used in the West: the methods of psychological suggestion and manipulation that give the individual the illusion of having and following his own convictions, while "his" decisions are in reality made by the élite of "decision makers."

The Russians believe that they represent socialism because they talk in terms of Marxist ideology, and they do not recognize how similar their system is to the most developed form of capitalism. We in the West believe that we represent the system of individualism, private initiative, and humanistic ethics, because we hold on to *our* ideology, and we do not see that our institutions are, in fact, in many ways becoming more and more similar to the hated system of communism. We believe that the essence of the Russian system is that the individual is subservient to the State, and hence that he has no freedom. But we do not recognize that in Western society the individual

[24] Benjamin A. Javits, l.c. p. 346.

is becoming more and more subservient to the economic machine, to the big corporation, to public opinion. We do not recognize that the individual, confronted with giant enterprises, giant government, giant trade unions, is afraid of freedom, has no faith in his own strength, and seeks shelter by identifying with these giants.

Our mode of industrial organization needs men similar to men the Soviet system needs: men who feel that they are the masters of their society (both capitalism and communism make this claim), yet who are willing to be commanded, to do what is expected of them, to fit into the social machine without friction and who can be guided without force, led without leaders, prompted without aim—except the one of making good, of being on the move, of getting ahead. We try to reach this result by means of the ideology of free enterprise, individual initiative, etc.; the Russians by the ideology of socialism, solidarity, and equality.

The question whether the Soviet system is a socialist system has been answered in the negative. We have concluded that it is a state managerialism, using the most advanced methods of total monopolization, centralization, mass manipulation, and moving slowly from exercising this manipulation by violence to exercising it by mass suggestion. It is, while resembling socialism in certain economic features, its very contradiction in a social and human sense, and is actually converging with the trends of the most advanced capitalistic countries, provided these do not change their present course. It is economically a very successful system, and while unfavorable to the development of authentic freedom and individualism, it has many features of planning and social welfare which can be counted as very positive achievements.

II) IS THE SOVIET UNION
A REVOLUTIONARY-IMPERIALIST SYSTEM?

The thesis that the aim of the Soviet Union is to dominate the world is based on two assumptions. The main one is that Khrushchev, being a communist and a successor of Lenin, wants to revolutionize the world for the victory of communism. The auxiliary assumption is that Khrushchev, as the successor of the Czars, is the leader of Russian imperialism, the aim of which is world domination. Sometimes the two assumptions are combined, sometimes it is even said that it is futile "to debate whether the Soviet Union is 'really' interested in world domination. For the problem may be that the Soviet conception of security results in undermining all other states."[25] Furthermore, there are also divided opinions about *how* the Soviet Union wants to achieve world domination. The opinion prevailing until recently—and maybe still today—is that the Soviet Union wants to conquer the world by the force of arms, while in view of Russian peace gestures the added assumption is frequently made that, if not by violence, the Soviet Union wants to achieve domination by economic means and nonviolent subversion.

Let us discuss these various views on the Soviet drive for world domination and examine the validity of the arguments in favor of the thesis.

a) The Soviet Union as a revolutionary power and the role of the Comintern

The oldest, and probably still the most popular concept is that of the continuity of the Lenin-Stalin-

[25] Cf. Henry A. Kissinger, *The Necessity of Choice*, Harper & Bros., New York, 1960, p. 149.

Khrushchev regimes and from the revolutionary communism of 1917–21 to Soviet power forty years later. Indeed, if Khrushchev were the legitimate successor of Lenin and a Communist in the Marx-Leninist tradition, his main interest would be the communization of the world; for, no doubt, Lenin hoped and worked for an international revolution, for the victory of communism—not of the Russian state—in the world.

But, as I have tried to show, Stalin and Khrushchev, all ideology to the contrary, do not represent revolutionary communism but a conservative, totalitarian managerialism, and the dominant class of this system. The question arises whether the representatives of this system and this class can be communist revolutionaries —whether they can desire, or even be in sympathy with, revolutions abroad, the spirit of which would be the opposite of that which dominates Russia.

The answer to this question depends on a more general political assumption, namely that the *internal structure of a regime determines its attitude toward revolutions.* A conservative power has by its very nature no use for revolutionary movements abroad. For one thing, the leaders of a conservative power are men who rule on the basis of authority and obedience, and revolutions are movements that fight authority and obedience. Those who come to power in conservative systems are, as persons, unsympathetic to anti-authoritarian attitudes. More important, however, is the fact that revolutions in other countries, especially if they are not too distant (geographically and culturally), constitute a threat to the conservative countries. This means, concretely, that if there were workers' revolutions in Berlin, West Germany, France, Italy, for example, the Soviet bureaucracy would have a difficult task in keeping these revolutions from spreading to East

Germany, Poland, Hungary, etc. At best the Soviet regime would have to use tanks and machine guns again, as it had to use them against the uprisings in East Germany, Poland, and Hungary to crush the uprising of the revolutionary workers. Would, or could, Khrushchev like this?

My thesis that the Soviet Union, being a conservative, hierarchical system, is against revolutions, will at first strike many readers as little better than nonsense. They will think of Lenin and Trotsky's hope for a world revolution, of Stalin's and Khrushchev's declarations about the "victory of communism," and of the conquest of the Baltic states, Poland, Czechoslovakia, Bulgaria, and Rumania by Russia. How, so they will argue, can one maintain that Khrushchevism is not a revolutionary system in view of all the obvious evidence to the contrary?

To answer this question, let us follow, step by step, the change from the genuine hope for a world revolution held by Lenin and his collaborators to the transformation of the Communist Parties into the instrument for Stalin's foreign policy.

There has always been ambiguity in the relationship between Russia and the international Communist movement. But the nature of this ambiguity changed drastically between 1917 and 1925. As I have pointed out, Lenin and Trotsky had believed that only a revolution in Germany (or Europe) could save the Russian revolution. Their foreign policy was subordinated to their revolutionary aims; but when the German revolution failed to materialize and Russia remained the only Communist country, she became the symbol and the center of the Communist hopes. The survival of Soviet Russia became a goal in itself although it was still believed that the survival of Russia was necessary for the final victory of communism. Yet, in a subtle way the interests of foreign Communist Parties began to be subordinated to the interests of Soviet foreign policy.

This development began as early as 1920. After the threat from the civil war and allied intervention had virtually been ended, there were first attempts to open negotiations with the West and to put the interest of the survival of the Russian state above that of world revolution. Chicherin sent out an appeal to the allied governments to enter into peace negotiations, and both he and Radek declared for the first time that capitalist states and Soviet Russia could peacefully coexist, just as "liberal England did not fight continuously against serf-owning Russia."[26] But the French-supported Polish attack on Russia and the initial Russian successes put a stop to this first appearance of the hope for coexistence. Instead, these events brought the revolutionary hopes of Lenin to a last intense climax. As I have pointed out, the disappointment of these hopes was virtually the end of Moscow's revolutionary strategy in the West.

The years 1921 and 1922 mark this end unmistakably. In 1921 the German Communist uprising was defeated, Lenin introduced the New Economic Policy or NEP, concluded a trade agreement with Great Britain, and suppressed the Kronstadt rebellion. Lenin and Trotsky did not give up their revolutionary hopes, but they acknowledged defeat. For the first time in the history of the Comintern, the suspicion was voiced both by Italian and by German Communists and left socialists, that there might be a latent contradiction between the interests of Russia and those of the Comintern and its member parties.[27]

[26] Cf. E. H. Carr, Vol. III, p. 161.
[27] Carr, l.c. pp. 395–96.

One of the first signs of the subordination of communism to Russian foreign policy may be seen in the new line of the German Communist Party (K.P.D.) about the time of the Rapallo treaty. While, until then, the K.P.D. had declined to support a German bourgeois government (as evidenced in its passive attitude toward the reactionary Kapp *Putsch*), between the summer of 1921 to the conclusion of the Rapallo pact in April 1922, a new attitude developed. The Communists supported the treaty in the Reichstag, and the *Rote Fahne* praised it as "the first independent act of foreign policy by the German bourgeoisie since 1918."[28] These events meant, writes Carr, "that among the most advanced Communist parties in the world, attitudes and policies would be different according to whether the governments of their respective countries were in hostile or friendly relations with the Soviet government, and would have to be modified from time to time, to take into account the changes in those relations. These consequences took a long time to develop fully, and were certainly not realized by those who made the Rapallo treaty in the spring of 1922."[29] Six months after Rapallo, the Soviet government made a second attempt for a comeback as a world power by its support of the Turks at the Lausanne conference; the persecution of the Communists in Turkey was no hindrance to the Russo-Turkish friendship.

By 1922 the failure of the revolutionary hopes was openly acknowledged. Radek declared at the IV Congress of the Comintern (November–December 1922): "The characteristic of the time in which we are living is that, although the crisis of world capital has not yet been overcome, although the question of power is still

[28] Quoted by E. H. Carr, l.c. Vol. III, p. 415.
[29] l.c. p. 415.

the centre of all questions, *the broadest masses of the proletariat have lost belief in their ability to conquer power in any forseeable time . . .* If that is the situation, if the great majority of the working class feels itself powerless, *then the conquest of power as an immediate task of the day is not on the agenda.*"[30] The speeches of Lenin and Zinoviev, while not as drastically pessimistic, were essentially in the same minor key.

What happened by 1922 is clearer for the historian today than it was for the participants in those events. The hope for the revolution had failed. Just as Marx and Engels in the middle of the nineteenth century had underestimated the vitality of capitalism, so Lenin and Trotsky between 1917 and 1922 had failed to recognize that the majority of the workers in the West were not willing to give up the economic and social advantages the capitalist system had provided for them for the dangerous and insecure course of a socialist revolution.

At first, in 1921 and 1922 the revolutionary retreat was made in good faith by Lenin and the other leaders. They made a strategic retreat and hoped that some time in the future a new revolutionary situation would arise. But with Lenin's illness and death, Trotsky's slow elimination, and Stalin's ascendancy, the retreat turned into a plain fraud. Although there is probably no single point at which this change could be said to have occurred, its development can be followed quite clearly in the sequence of events from the Rapallo pact in 1922 to the pact with Hitler in 1939.

[30] Protokoll des IV Kongresses der Kommunistischen Internationale, Hamburg, 1923, p. 33, quoted by E. H. Carr, l.c. Vol. III, p. 444.

After the *Putsch* in Germany in 1923, through which "Communist prestige suffered a new and this time an irreparable blow"[31] Stalin's view of the supremacy of Russia's national interests over the revolutionary interests of the communist parties gained steady ascendency. He always had contempt for foreign Communist Parties and expressed this contempt many times. "The Comintern represents nothing. It exists only because of our support,"[32] he said to Lominadze in the twenties. The same attitude was expressed many years later when he said to the Polish leader Mikolajczyk "communism fits Germany as a saddle fits a cow."[33] His personal contempt for the Chinese Communists was notorious. Under him, the relationship between Russia and the Communist movement changed drastically; the might of Russia was the goal, and the Communist Parties had to serve this goal.

For the first time Stalin acknowledged officially in 1925 that the acute revolutionary period after the First World War had passed and was being followed by a period of "relative stabilization." Only in 1947 did he publish a speech to Communist students that he made in 1925, which throws a retrospective light on his attitude: "I suppose that the revolutionary forces of the West are great; that they grow; that they will grow, and that they may overthrow the *bourgeoisie* here or there. That is true. But it will be very difficult for them to hold their ground . . . The problem of our army, of its strength and readiness, will inevitably arise in connection with complications in the countries that surround us . . . This does not mean that in any such

[31] George F. Kennan, *Soviet Foreign Policy, 1917–1941*, l.c. p. 49.
[32] Quoted by Isaac Deutscher, l.c. p. 392.
[33] Quoted by Isaac Deutscher, l.c. p. 537.

situation we are bound in duty to intervene actively against anybody."[34]

This statement is a good example of the difference between ritualistic language and real policy which would from then on pervade all Russian statements. The expressions of hope in the growth of the revolutionary forces are the ritual, without which no Communist statement could be made, but the operative part of the statement lies in the point that Stalin evaded any commitment that the Red Army would come out to help foreign revolutions hold their ground. He left this open, but insisted that he was not "bound in duty" to intervene.

Russia's foreign policy seemed to be successful for a while in the attempt to open friendly relations with the West, especially with Great Britain. But the British conservative government moved clearly toward a break with Russia between 1924 and 1927. The Soviet Trade Delegation in London was raided on May 12, 1927, and, although the raid apparently did not yield any very incriminating evidence, the British government nevertheless severed all official relations with Russia on May 26, 1927.[35] After this setback in its foreign policy, "the Soviet government turned its back even more resolutely than before on actual revolutionary activities abroad, retired into a semi-isolation, and devoted its efforts to the accomplishment of two great internal programs."[36] These two programs were the rapid industrialization of Russia, expressed in the first Five Year Plan, 1928–33, and the establishment of a tight control over Russian agriculture. Trotsky was expelled from the party, and Stalin began the construc-

[34] Quoted by I. Deutscher, l.c. p. 411.
[35] Cf. George F. Kennan, l.c. p. 63.
[36] l.c. p. 77.

tion of a Russian managerial industrialism. As George Kennan has pointed out, this new program demanded tremendous sacrifices from the Russian population, and Stalin, as a justification for these hardships, had to emphasize the appearance of an external danger.[37] He also used radical phraseology to hide the final abandonment of the revolutionary ideas and, in addition, to show the Western powers the nuisance value of the Communist Parties as a response to their hostile reaction after 1924.

These three motives explain the new militant course of the Comintern after 1927. Stalin declared in his report on December 3, 1927, that "the stabilization of capitalism is becoming more and more rotten and unstable."[38] The official Comintern line was changed to say that the capitalist world had now entered upon another "cycle of wars and revolutions." This new "revolutionary" line has been often interpreted by American Sovietologists as a proof that Stalinism never relinquished its revolutionary plans. These observers do not see that this radical line was purely in the service of Russian foreign and internal policy, and not the expression of any genuine revolutionary plans.

The best over-all judgment on the new revolutionary line is presented by Gustav Hilger, the Counselor of the German Embassy in Moscow at the time. "Thus a competent Moscow observer of that day," writes Kennan, "was able later, in describing Soviet policy during the first Five Year Plan period, to say that the Soviet Union 'concealed an ironclad isolationism behind a façade of intensified Comintern activity which was designed in part to detract attention from her in-

[37] l.c. p. 79.
[38] Quoted by George Kennan, l.c. p. 164.

ternal troubles.' "[39] It must be noted furthermore that in spite of all radical talk, the Comintern did not send out any directives that demanded the seizure of power, but demanded only the continued struggle against "the capitalist offensive."[40]

With the consolidation of Stalin's power over all opponents, Hitler's accession to power, and the beginning of the Roosevelt era, Stalin ordered another switch. He did not try to mobilize the German workers against Hitler with the goal of establishing a leftist government in Germany. On the contrary, led by a Moscow stooge who was treated with complete contempt by the Moscow bosses, the K.P.D. was told to follow a policy which was plainly suicidal. Treating the socialists as their main enemies and making a tactical pact with the Nazis, the Communist Party did everything possible *not* to prevent a Nazi victory. It is unthinkable that Stalin would have demoralized and stultified the German Communist Party so completely had his aim been a revolution in Germany, or even the defeat of Hitler. In saying this I do not mean to imply that Stalin wished for Hitler's victory. He certainly saw himself threatened by Hitler and tried his best to avert this threat. But

[39] George F. Kennan, l.c. p. 80, quoting Gustav Hilger and Alfred G. Meyer, *The Incompatible Allies*, The Macmillan Co., New York, 1953, p. 225.

[40] Capitalist Stabilization has Ended, Thesis and Resolutions of the Twelfth Plenum of the Ex. Comm. of the Comintern. Workers Library Publ. New York, 1932, p. 7, quoted by H. Marcuse, l.c. p. 54. Cf. also Marcuse's analysis of the 1927 line. "Thus," he summarizes, "even the most 'leftist' Communist program does not contradict our assumption that Stalinist strategy implied *effective containment of the revolutionary potential in the Western world after the failure of the Central European revolutions.*"

there are many good reasons—although no conclusive proof—to think that Stalin preferred the victory of Hitler to an authentic worker's revolution in Germany. The German dictator was a military threat with which Stalin could hope to cope with diplomatic maneuvers and military preparation. A German workers' revolution would have undermined the basis of his whole regime.

Stalin's attempts to arrive at an anti-Nazi coalition with the West were supported by new orders to the foreign Communist Parties. They were told to take the line of co-operation with liberal and democratic elements in their respective countries, and to form a united front with all "anti-fascist" elements, including the Social Democrats. This policy was officially sanctioned at the VIII (and last) Comintern Congress, 1935.

Stalin's foreign policy did not succeed, in spite of the new Comintern line. "In many capitals, and not least in London, there were serious inhibitions about any policy of collaboration with Soviet Russia, even for the containment of fascism. The League of Nations, reflecting these inhibitions, proved a feeble and ineffective reed. The final language of the Franco-Soviet Pact was complicated and vague, and its operation was made extensively contingent on prior action by the League of Nations. It was not followed up (until 1939, when it was much too late) by any concrete military discussions. The French government, finally, delayed so long with its ratification, and exhibited so many hesitations in the process, that its value as a political demonstration was reduced to almost negligible proportions. The contempt of the Germans for its existence was clearly demonstrated by the reoccupation of the Rhineland in March 1936; and the failure of the western powers to react with any strong measures showed how ineffective was the Pact for the purposes Moscow had had in mind in concluding it."[41]

The Spanish Civil War, in which the West helped in the defeat of the Republican government by an arms embargo while at the same time not seriously interfering with the military aid sent to Franco by Hitler and Mussolini, could not encourage Stalin's hope. Yet even here his actions were far from revolutionary. After some hesitation at the beginning of the Franco rebellion, the Russians decided to intervene, since Franco's victory "would have meant the encirclement of France by the fascists, the probable triumph of fascist tendencies within France herself, and the further weakening of Western resistance to Hitler. The way would then be clear for German aggression toward the East."[42]

Russia sent military help, but reconciled herself to the Republic's defeat when it became clear that only a much larger amount of Russian assistance could counteract the Italian-German support. While Soviet military aid began to taper off in 1937, Stalin continued to exterminate his socialist and anarchist rivals in Spain. When the destruction of his political rivals (who—against the Russian view—wanted to transform the civil war into a fight for socialism), conflicted with the demands of the war effort, "precedence was given quite ruthlessly by the Kremlin to the first of these two requirements, to the embitterment of the Spanish Republican leaders."[43]

Most of those Communist generals and functionaries who had fought in Spain were executed in Russia soon

[41] George F. Kennan, l.c. p. 86.
[42] l.c. p. 87.
[43] l.c. p. 89.

after their return. Stalin wanted to eliminate all elements who by their acquaintance with Western revolutionary ideas stood in the way of the final liquidation of the revolutionary tradition which he undertook in those years of the purges. In short, Stalin's attitude toward Franco was similar to his attitude toward Hitler. He would have preferred the downfall of Franco, but not at the price of a popular revolution in Spain, which might have become the signal for revolutionary uprisings in other European countries.

When Stalin's attempts to come to an arrangement with the West had failed (and it is not too far-fetched to speculate that his destruction of almost all of the leading Communists of the Lenin era was his final attempt to show the West that he was not encumbered by his revolutionary past), Stalin changed his course again, this time by concluding a pact with the Nazis. Immediately, the Communist Parties followed suit. Molotov had given the cue with his statement that "Nazism was a matter of taste." The Communists changed their anti-fascist line and began to attack the "Western imperialists." As a gesture of friendship toward Nazism, German Communist refugees in Russia were delivered to Hitler's Gestapo, if there were any doubts about their loyalty to the new party line. The Comintern took a line of neutrality toward the two camps.

The core of this new Comintern policy between the Soviet-Nazi pact and the German attack on Russia has been described very succinctly by Deutscher: "Both belligerent camps, it was now said, pursued imperialist aims, and there was nothing to choose between them. The working classes were called upon to resist war and fight for peace. Outwardly, these appeals resembled the policy of revolutionary defeatism which Lenin had pursued in the First World War. The resemblance was deceptive. In Lenin's opposition to war there was revolutionary integrity and consistency, while the policy of the Comintern merely suited the temporary convenience of Stalin's diplomacy and was as tortuous as that diplomacy. At times the opposition to war had an unmistakably pro-German twist as, for instance, in October 1939, when the Comintern echoed Molotov's and von Ribbentrop's call for a negotiated peace and blamed France and Britain for the war. The effect of that policy, especially in France, was merely defeatist, not revolutionary. It supplemented the defeatism that corroded the top of French society with a quasi-popular brand of defeatism coming from below. Only after the harm had been done, when Moscow, alarmed by Hitler's victories, began to encourage resistance to Nazi occupation, did the French Communist Party switch over to a new policy. Less obvious, though not unimportant, was the effect of the von Ribbentrop-Molotov pact upon anti-Nazi elements in Germany; it made their confusion worse confounded, it deepened their sense of defeat and induced some of them to reconcile themselves to Hitler's war."[44]

With the German attack against Russia, the line of the Communist Parties shifted again to give support to Russia. The French Communists were told to join the resistance movement, and the slogans of the period after 1933 were revived. Clearly, Stalin did not try to use the war as a springboard for a revolution in the West. Quite the contrary, especially in Italy and France, where the Communists by their participation in the resistance movement had gained general pres-

[44] Isaac Deutscher's *Stalin,* Vintage Books, New York, 1960.

tige and influence, Stalin did everything to prove that these Communist Parties had no revolutionary aim. They surrendered their arms and "for the first time in their history, disregarding their own programs, which forbade them to take part in bourgeois administrations, they joined in governments based on broad national coalitions. Although they were then the strongest parties in their countries, they contented themselves with minor positions in those governments, from which they could not hope to seize power either now or later and from which they were eventually to be ousted, almost without effort, by the other parties. The army and the police remained in the hands of Conservative or, at any rate, anti-Communist groups. Western Europe was to remain the domain of Liberal capitalism."[45]

In Italy even much later the Communist deputies, against the Socialist and Liberal votes, voted for the renewal of the Lateran pacts, which Mussolini had concluded with the Vatican. In Greece, during the uprising of 1944-48, Stalin upheld the Yalta decision according to which Greece was to remain in the Western sphere of interest,[46] and in consequence he did not assist the Greek Communists by military intervention.

Those who claim that Stalin wanted to conquer the world for the Comintern could hardly answer the question why after the war, with armed and enthusiastic Communists in Italy and France, he did not issue the call for revolution and support it by an invasion of Russian troops; why, instead, he proclaimed a period of "capitalist stabilization" and had the Communist Parties follow a policy of co-operation and a "minimum program," which never had as its aim a Communist revolution.

[45] Deutscher, l.c. p. 518.
[46] Cf. David J. Dallin, l.c. p. 14.

George Kennan arrives basically at the same conclusion when he writes that Stalin "was generally hesitant to encourage foreign Communist Parties to attempt to seize power,"[47] although he arrives at this conclusion on different grounds—which I also subscribe to—namely, Stalin's fear that domestic rivals could make common cause against him with the leaders of strong foreign Communist Parties.

After 1946 the relations between the East and the West began to freeze. The West had disarmed and became suspicious of aggressive Russian designs on the whole Western world when Stalin, violating the Yalta agreements, installed his regimes in Poland, Hungary, Rumania, and Bulgaria. Churchill, in his Fulton, Missouri, speech, voiced this Western apprehension and this, apparently, Stalin understood to be the spectrum of a new Western alliance against the Soviet Union. This fear of a Western alliance against the Soviets had always dominated Stalin's mind. It was by no means only a tactical excuse, nor was it entirely unrealistic; although in 1946 it was much greater than the facts warranted. On the other hand, the West was always suspicious of Russian schemes for world revolutionary conquests, and Stalin's actions after the war seemed to confirm the worst. Thus, based on mutual suspicions, which were mainly unrealistic at the time, the cold war started. Stalin reacted to the stiffening attitude of the West by an aggressive Russian strategy in 1947–48 (the establishment of the Cominform in 1947, the coup in Czechoslovakia, the Berlin blockade, and the break with Tito in 1948). But at the same time, the chief Soviet economic theoretician, Varga, was permitted to publish his analysis of the development of capitalism, in which he recognized in a cautious way

[47] George F. Kennan, l.c. p. 54.

the stabilizing and productive functions of capitalism. Even though his theories were rejected, their publication in the highly controlled Stalinist system was a straw in the wind. Since then, Soviet ideology has re-emphasized (both in 1956 and in 1958) the older theory that the inherent contradictions within the capitalist system are the determining factors in the evolution of capitalism. This theory implies that there is no reason for serious revolutionary activities in the Western countries since they will eventually fall under the weight of these inherent contradictions. (I shall discuss the ideological character of this theory later; suffice it to say here that the *operative* part of this formulation is that there is no need for revolutionary action while the *ritualistic part* is the hope for Communist revolution.)

The principles of the 1956 liberalization were repeated and reinforced in the statement of the representatives of 81 Communist Parties, Moscow, November 1960.[48] This statement, which bears the imprint of Khrushchev's views in all essential questions rather than those of the Chinese Communists declares: "The course of social development proves right Lenin's prediction *that the countries of victorious socialism would influence the development of world revolution chiefly by their economic construction. Socialism has made unprecedented constructive progress in production, science and technology and in the establishment of a new, free community of people, in which their material and spiritual requirements are increasingly satisfied.*

"The time is not far off when socialism's share of world production will be greater than that of capital-

[48] Published in *The New York Times*, December 7, 1960 (my italics, E.F.).

ism. Capitalism will be defeated in the decisive sphere of human endeavor, the sphere of material production.

"The consolidation and development of the socialist system exert an ever-increasing influence on the structure of the peoples in the capitalist countries. By the force of its example, the world socialist system in revolutionizing the thinking of the working people in the capitalist countries, it is inspiring them to fight against capitalism, and is greatly facilitating that fight."

The statement declares furthermore that "In a world divided into two systems, the only correct and reasonable principle of international relations is the principle of *peaceful coexistence of states with different social systems* advanced by Lenin and further elaborated in the Moscow Declaration and the Peace Manifesto of 1957, in the decisions of the Twentieth and Twenty-first Congresses of the C.P.S.U., and in the documents of other Communist and workers' parties." And another time, Khrushchev's argument is repeated: "Peaceful coexistence of countries with different systems or destructive war—this is the alternative today. There is no other choice. Communists emphatically reject the U.S. doctrine of cold war and brinkmanship, for it is a policy leading to thermonuclear catastrophe.

"By upholding the principle of peaceful coexistence, the Communists fight for the *complete cessation of the cold war,* dismantling of military bases, for general and complete disarmament, under international control, the settlement of international disputes through negotiation, respect for the equality of states and their territorial integrity, independence and sovereignty, non-interference in each others' internal affairs, extensive development of trade, cultural and scientific ties between nations."

Clearly we find here the same phenomenon that has

taken place again and again since the twenties. Khrushchev wants peace with the West, and Communist policies are geared to this Russian policy. However, there is one fundamental difference between the period before the Second World War and the sixties. Stalin reigned supreme over foreign Communists, and gave them his orders. With the rise of Communist China, Khrushchev has to reckon with an influential rival, for whom revolutionary slogans and aggressive aims are more than mere ritualistic declarations. This rival has its own allies within the international Communist movement, and probably also within the Soviet Union. Khrushchev's peace policy must succeed—or he will lose out against his rivals.[49]

b) The Soviet Union as an imperialist power

Even though the Soviet Union may not be a revolutionary power, is she not an imperialist power and as such is not her aim one of world domination? The conquest of the satellite states is referred to as the first step toward such designs.

(Clearly, the conquest of the satellite states can hardly be considered a revolutionary accomplishment. They were won not by workers' revolutions, but by Russian military occupation. They were, especially at first, nothing but conquered states forced to adopt the conqueror's social and political system.)[50]

[49] The political attitude of Khrushchev has been very succinctly described by Walter Lippmann in his report on his interview with Khrushchev in April 1961. "Mr. Khrushchev thinks much more like Richelieu and Metternich than like Woodrow Wilson."

[50] The only satellite state that was the result of an authentic Communist-national revolution and not of Russian occupation, Yugoslavia, asserted its complete independence from Russia in 1948.

Indeed, at Yalta, Stalin had approved the common declaration which stipulated: "To foster the conditions in which the liberated peoples may exercise these rights, the three governments will jointly assist the people in any European liberated state or former Axis satellite state in Europe where in their judgment conditions require (a) to establish conditions of internal peace; (b) to carry out emergency measures for the relief of distressed peoples; (c) to form interim governmental authorities broadly representative of all democratic elements in the population and pledged to the earliest possible establishment through free elections of governments responsive to the will of the people; and (d) to facilitate where necessary the holding of such elections." Stalin broke his promise, and made these states his sphere of interest. What were his reasons?

I believe Z. K. Brzezinski has given a correct answer in the following paragraphs: "The immediate objectives dictating the Soviet policy in East Europe during the war and immediately afterwards, and affecting the pattern of Soviet relations with it, may be broken down into five major areas of presumed Soviet interest. The first involved the desire to exert influence on the lands immediately west of the Russian frontier in order to deny the area to Germany—in the past a source of major threat to Russian security. There is no doubt that from the perspective of the *prenuclear* age the Soviet leaders could not feel certain that the mere defeat of Germany would ensure Soviet security and that the post-World War I situation would not be repeated. Moscow's emphasis on security was readily understood by the Western powers, especially in view of Russia's war effort. Prime Minister Winston Churchill frequently stated in the Commons during the war that the

West was willing to go to some lengths to guarantee Soviet security from Germany on terms satisfactory to the Russians. As a result, the Western leaders were also inclined to grant the Soviet Union the benefit of the doubt insofar as the second broad Soviet objective was concerned: to ensure that East Europe would not be controlled by domestic elements which, while hostile to Germany, would also be hostile to the Soviet Union. Stalin encountered little difficulty in demonstrating that East Europe could not shield the USSR against a resurgent Germany if simultaneously it was unwilling to collaborate very closely with the USSR.[51] Hence, he argued, it is essential that East Europe not only be denied to Germany but also that it be governed by regimes which were purged of all opponents of the USSR. Given the prevailing power balance, it was up to Stalin to decide what criteria would determine just who was an enemy of the USSR.

"The remaining three probable Soviet objectives for East Europe seemed at the time less apparent to the West; or perhaps it was that the West simply felt unable to oppose them. The first of these was to use the area for purposes of Soviet economic recovery. The war damages inflicted on the USSR by the Germans could be healed much more rapidly by extracting capital from East Central Europe through the removal of enterprises and resources. Insofar as the former Axis powers were concerned—that is Bulgaria, Hungary, and Rumania as well as Germany—the Western powers concurred and a policy of reparations was endorsed. The situation differed sharply in the case of Poland,

[51] This attitude of refusal to cooperate with the Soviet Union was taken by the Polish government shortly before Poland was invaded by Germany. (E.F.)

Czechoslovakia, and Yugoslavia, all Allied powers. There could be no question of direct reparations, but at least in the case of Poland and Yugoslavia the Soviet Union extracted some economic advantages. In Poland there was the matter of the incorporation of eastern Poland into the USSR and the removal of industrial equipment from those parts of Germany assigned to Poland as compensation for the German occupation and for the loss of territory to the USSR. In the case of Yugoslavia joint companies were established which, according to the Yugoslavs, the USSR found profitable.

"The fourth objective, we may surmise, was to deny the area to the capitalist world since it was likely to plot hostile moves against the USSR. No doubt the Soviet leaders, even at the height of the Grand Alliance, must have considered the possibility that some day after the conclusion of the war the capitalist world would again be arrayed against the USSR.[52] Many of the wartime Soviet suspicions about alleged British or American contacts with German anti-Nazi groups were derived from such general ideological assumptions about capitalist behavior. As a result, Anglo-American declarations to the effect that postwar governments in East Central Europe must be democratic were presumably viewed in Moscow with a great deal of mistrust. The Kremlin undoubtedly suspected that such governments were meant to be the springboard for an eventual capitalist onslaught against the USSR.

"The fifth probable objective was related to the preceding one. If ideological assumptions played a role in the crystallization of Soviet defensive interests in East Europe, then it is likely that the other part of the

[52] Cf. for Stalin's suspicions of Western alliance against him George Kennan's book, l.c. p. 172.

ideological orientation, namely its offensive compo-
nent, was also present. Leninist-Stalinist strategic concepts have always emphasized the importance of a
strong basis for expansive operation, and it is inevitable
that any accretion of territory to the base of socialism
in itself was regarded as reflecting the march of socialism toward its eventual victory. It would be impossible
not to relate the new political situation in East Europe
to this historical process, especially since the prevailing situation was already clearly suggesting that the
area had become divorced from capitalist domination
in space and from the capitalist era in time. It would
be inconceivable not to consider the establishment of
Soviet power in East Europe as another revolutionary
turning point in a process which *must go forward*."[53]

As far as Brzezinski's fifth point is concerned, it needs
some qualifications. There is no doubt that Stalin
wanted to show himself, true to the ideology, as the
revolutionary successor of Lenin, and as a successful
statesman, but it is equally clear that in the case of
the satellites he was a successor of the Czars, rather
than of Lenin and Trotsky. Aside from this, the first
four points mentioned by Brzezinski are quite sufficient to explain Stalin's conquests of these states, and
the fact that they were objectives which as such had
nothing to do with communism, world revolution, etc.

---

[53] Z. K. Brzezinski *The Soviet Bloc*, Harvard University
Press, Cambridge, Mass., 1960, pp. 4–6. Brzezinski's
third point is strengthened by data given by Herbert Feis
(*Churchill–Roosevelt–Stalin*, Princeton University Press,
Princeton, New Jersey, 1957) and William Appelman Wil-
liams (*The Tragedy of American Diplomacy*, World Publishing Company, Cleveland, 1959) who both point to the
American reluctance to aid Russia's post-war reconstruc-
tion.

The wish to make these states a part of the Soviet sphere of interest would have existed equally in a Czarist or in a liberal government.

In the West this breach of promise was generally interpreted not only as a sign of Stalin's untrustworthiness, but also as a proof of his intention to conquer Europe, and later the world. Actually his action was, in principle, not different from the attitude of the British, French, and Italian leaders after the First World War at Versailles. In spite of having accepted Wilson's Fourteen Points, they insisted, under various rationalizations, on territorial acquisitions agreed on during the war in secret treaties, which made a mockery of Wilson's principles of self-determination. They wanted their spoils of war and they defeated Wilson. What Stalin did was essentially the same, and he too used various tricks to rationalize his breach of promise. He may, in fact, have thought that Roosevelt and Churchill had not meant the Yalta declaration to be entirely serious, and he may have been surprised when he discovered their genuine indignation. The question is: If the seizure of the satellite states was not a revolutionary action, was it an act of Russian imperialism, indicating a Russian desire for world conquest?

No doubt the Soviet Union is the heir to Czarist Russia. As I indicated before, the industrial development of a potentially rich country like Russia must have led to the emergence of a strong, industrial Russia under any ideology provided she were led by a government capable of chosing adequate methods for its economic development.

Czarist Russia was an imperialist power, as were Great Britain, France, and Germany. Her main aspirations were to gain a warm water port (preferably through control of the Dardanelles), control of Persia (in 1907 Czarist Russia agreed to share with Great Britain the control of Persia), and spheres of influence in the Near, Middle, and Far East. The Russian government was not particularly successful in its attempts for territorial aggrandizement, especially after the loss of the war against Japan in 1905. But quite aside from this, Czarist imperialism was bound by the same limitations as that of the other European countries.

What were these limitations? The first and essential point to remember is that European imperialism of the nineteenth century never aimed at *world domination*. The study of European diplomatic history from the middle of the nineteenth century to the beginning of the First World War shows quite clearly that because of economic interests, and reasons of security and prestige, each power wanted new spheres of interest; that there was intensive competition, intrigues, and secret deals, which would be called subversive today provided the Soviet Union were the culprit; but there was no serious attempt to dominate the world. Even the Kaiser and Hitler, in spite of their aggressive postures, never dreamed of world domination. Hitler, in his most expansionist periods, never wanted more than hegemony over Western Europe and certain territory at the expense of Czechoslovakia, Poland, and Russia. Neither England nor the United States was ever included in his dreams of empire. True enough, Hitler's soldiers sang "Morgen Gehört Uns die Ganze Welt" ("Tomorrow the Whole World Will Belong to Us"), but that was in the realm of nationalist ideology, no more serious than his "socialist" promises. In spite of his half-madness, Hitler was sufficiently realistic (and also sufficiently under the control of his industrialist and military "advisers") to know that world conquest was not feasible even though he may have dreamed about it.

Is world domination the aim of the Soviet Union?

Not only did none of the Western imperialist powers aim at world domination, their diplomats were also most eager not to pursue their limited aims beyond a point at which a major war could be provoked. In 1914 this peace strategy collapsed, although it is still open to debate whether the war was really "necessary" or whether it was the result of stupid bungling on all sides.

However this may be, the point I want to stress is that imperialism is not the same as a drive for "world domination," and that, in as much as Russia is the successor of Czarist imperialism, this does not make her into a power that wants to conquer the world. I have pointed out before that Russia's conquest of the satellites was a limited big power grab, carried out for economic and security reasons, at a time when Stalin thought he could get away with it. But on the whole the Soviet Union has shown no more expansionism than the limited one of the imperialism of the Western powers. The reasons are quite obvious. Russia, being a tremendous territory, needs neither raw materials nor markets. She is in this respect in a position similar to that of the United States, which, in spite of some imperialistic actions (Cuba, the Philippines), did not need to conquer new territories. Furthermore, in the nuclear age the leaders of the Soviet Union have even a great deal more reason to avoid a major war than had the statesmen of Europe in the nineteenth century.

However, all these considerations remain rather theoretical unless they are borne out by the record of the Soviet Union's political behavior. We have already dealt with the postwar conquests of the satellite states. There is a second attempt at expansion of Russia's sphere of interest, the attack against South Korea. It must be noted that this was originally a Russian-sponsored, not a Chinese, attack and that it was probably aimed as much against China as against the United States.[54] (A glance at a map shows the strategic importance that Korea has for the Russian position in the Far East.) Stalin may have been misled by Dean Acheson's declaration, which omitted Korea from a list of those countries that the United States was prepared to defend, and furthermore by the fact that of the money allotted to Congress for the defense of Korea hardly any had been spent at the time of the attack. Stalin miscalculated badly; the United States fought back, and the Chinese (as a result of a United States miscalculation of the effect of going beyond the 38th parallel) came into the war and gained self-confidence and prestige by their capacity to contain the Western forces at the old dividing line.

No doubt the conquest of the satellites and the Korean War were expansionist, aggressive actions.[55] What about the rest of the Russian record? The Soviet Union, as I said before, not only did not take advantage of the postwar situation in France and Italy, she also did not undertake offensive action, nor try to put governments under her yoke where she could have done so without any great risk. Finland, Austria, Greece, Turkey, Iran, Iraq, Lebanon, Egypt, Cambodia, Laos are examples of Soviet policy that either left the respective countries in the Western orbit or neutral.

This picture is quite in contrast to the current cliché

[54] Cf. Louis Fischer, *Russia, America and the World*, l.c. p. 57.

[55] The same holds true for the incorporation of the Baltic states, parts of Poland and the territorial conquests in Finland in 1940. But in all these instances, Stalin was acting from strategic considerations and these conquests of former Czarist territories, while typically imperialist moves, were not the first steps to world domination.

that states that Berlin, Laos, the Congo, and Cuba are signs of Russia's aggressive wish to dominate the world. If this view were correct, our previous conclusions would have to be abandoned. Hence, we must deal with this argument in some detail.

I shall deal with Berlin in a later chapter. Suffice it to suggest at this point that the Soviet Union's policy is strategically speaking a defensive one; she wants recognition of the Western borders of her sphere of influence (including East Germany), and she wants to prevent West Germany's rearmament. The issue of Berlin is used tactically to prod the Western Allies into making concessions with regard to the first two issues, but there is no evidence that the Soviet Union intends to make West Berlin part of the Eastern zone. As far as Laos is concerned, the situation is basically that the Soviet Union wanted a neutralized Laos, and that the Western powers had agreed to a neutral commission to supervise Laos' neutrality. After a while, the United States tried to get Laos into the Western camp, and rejected the neutral commission. When the Soviet Union reacted by supporting the Communist elements in Laos, we protested against the Russian aggression. Apparently the Russians are quite willing to return to the original agreement about the neutralization of Laos. (It must be mentioned that here, as in many other parts of the world, the Russians are competing with the Chinese, and that some of the Russian actions have more the purpose of containing the Chinese, than of conquering new territories.)[56]

[56] Cf. the following description of the Laos situation, which differs radically from the cliché current in most of our utterances, made by the *Newsweek* veteran Southeast Asiatic correspondent, Robert S. Elegant (*Newsweek*, May 15, 1961): "The first big factor our policy-makers ignored

What about the Congo? In spite of a United Nations decision, the Belgians kept their foothold in the rich Katanga province and, one must surmise, engineered a military coup which overthrew the legitimate Lumumba government. Immediately afterward, the Russian mission was given by the Kasavubu government twenty-four hours notice to leave the Congo—and left. The Belgian officers continued to command the forces

---

was that landlocked Laos is vital to China's security. Any attempt to transform Laos into an anti-Communist bastion was doomed to failure from the start. Yet the U.S. sought to do this—with the worst possible tools. Our allies, the traditional ruling class, had little interest in reform. The political methods they used—stuffing ballot boxes and intimidating neutralist voters—succeeded only in driving the moderates to the left.

"It was the same with our aid program: The great bulk of it was used to build up a motorized army (in an almost roadless land), whose enlisted men often had to wait for months to draw their pay, while their generals lived in luxury. Funds for economic improvements were also frittered away. For instance, in 1960, only $590,750 out of $7 million was allotted for aid to agriculture in a country 99 percent agricultural, whereas better than $4 million went for salaries and upkeep of the American-aid personnel.

"The worst thing perhaps was that U.S. policy-makers never came to terms with any elements in Laos other than those they considered militantly anti-Communist. This policy led the CIA to back an army rebellion, led by Gen. Phoumi Nosavan, against the legitimate but neutralist government of Prince Souvanna Phouma. The army—and the right-wingers—won but in so doing drove other important groups into a fighting coalition that accepted Red support and now is on its way to power. The likeliest head of this coalition, which includes the Communists, is the man the U.S. spurned—Prince Souvanna Phouma."

of Tschombe in Katanga province, Kasavubu delivered
Lumumba to Tschombe to be murdered there, and
none of the Western powers exercised enough pressure
to prevent this from happening. The Russians suffered
a rather severe diplomatic defeat, which must have
constituted a serious setback for Khrushchev, all the
more so because the Chinese were quite active themselves in the Congo and could blame Khrushchev for
the failure of his policy. The West succeeded in ex-
cluding the Soviet Union completely from any influence
in the Congo, but there is no evidence that Russia was
more aggressive than to send fifteen commercial airplanes there. It seems that a rational solution would
have kept the Congo free from further Belgian domination, would have effectively guaranteed its independence by the United Nations, and would not have ex-
cluded the Soviet Union so brusquely from having any
influence in the newly created states.

Cuba is no better proof of Russian plans to dominate
the world.[57] The Cuban revolution was neither insti-
gated by Moscow nor by the Cuban Communists, who
had been collaborating with Batista until his downfall
was near. Castro was never a Communist, but he
planned a revolution which transcended the purely political limits of freeing the country from dictatorship.
He started a social revolution, expropriating land owners and industry. United States government and public
opinion started to turn against him, and forced Castro
step by step to seek help, economically and politically,
from the Soviet Union and to accept the help of the
Cuban Communist Party which had been held in contempt by the Castristas because of its obvious opportun-
ism and corruption.

[57] A more detailed discussion of the Cuban situation follows later on pp. 242–48.

Khrushchev threatened once to defend Cuba with nuclear bombs against American military intervention, when he knew quite well that the United States would not intervene in such a direct fashion. To make sure, he later withdrew this threat by declaring it was meant only symbolically.[58] He has given only the minimum of aid and loans to the Cubans, and it seems that he exercised a restraining influence on Castro, which, after Guevara's return from Moscow, led to repeated— though rejected—bids for a "new beginning" in Cuban-American relations. In Cuba too, Khrushchev has to cope with Chinese competition, which deprives him of some freedom of action. But the total picture shows that Castro, not Khrushchev, started the revolution, and that Castro's alliance with the Soviet Union was furthered more by United States action than by Khrushchev's wish to penetrate Latin America.

No doubt Khrushchev wants to keep the Communist Parties in Latin America alive for their nuisance value against the United States. He must give some support to them because of his position as leader in the Communist camp, (especially in view of the Chinese competition), but there is no evidence that Khrushchev has a serious wish to destroy all possibilities of an understanding with the United States by trying to make Latin America part of his empire.

To sum up: the cliché of the Soviet offensive against the United States in Berlin, Laos, the Congo, and Cuba is not based on reality but is rather a convenient formula to support further armament and the continuation of

[58] At the time of revising this manuscript (end of April 1961) Khrushchev, in spite of the American-supported invasion, did not repeat his earlier threat but declared only that he would help Cuba to defend itself—which is quite a different story.

the cold war. It corresponds to the Chinese cliché that pictures the United States as seeking world domination by the support of Chiang Kai-shek, by the domination of Southern Korea and Okinawa, by the SEATO pact, etc. All these mutual accusations can not stand up to sober and realistic analysis.

Kissinger expressed the view that it does not really matter whether the Soviet Union wants to dominate the world, because even if she wanted to undermine all non-Communist countries for reasons of security the result would be the same. Such a view leads from the realm of analysis of political reality to the realm of fantasy. It remains a mystery why, considering the relative equality of power now, the Soviet Union would have to conquer the rest of the world in order to be secure, especially when it is clear that before she took the first steps on this road a nuclear war would break out which would be the end of all "security."

Considering the Soviet Union's very limited form of imperialism, several considerations must be added. It has become customary to prove the Soviet Union's unlimited imperialism by counting China with her 600,-000,000 inhabitants as another proof of Russian aggrandizement. Anybody familiar with the facts knows, of course, that this is sheer nonsense. The Chinese revolution is authentically Chinese; it triumphed in spite of Stalin's conviction that it could not do so, and China received, as I shall show later, only a limited amount of aid from Russia, even after the Communists had won. The Chinese-Russian alliance was logical for both sides, but it has also its serious problems, especially for the Russians. To consider China a "conquest" of Russia is nothing but a demagogic formula.

What about the attitude of the Soviet Union toward the Communist Parties and toward national revolutions in the underdeveloped countries other than the nations we have already discussed? As far as the *Communist Parties* in the underdeveloped countries are concerned, part of their function is to serve as auxiliary forces for Russian foreign policy just as the Communist Parties do in the West. However, as far as *revolutions* in the underdeveloped countries are concerned, there is a considerable difference. While Stalin definitely did not want Communist revolutions in the West, he, just as Khrushchev is, was in favor of national revolutions in Asia and Africa. These national revolutions in underdeveloped countries are not a threat to the conservative Soviet regime, as Western workers' revolutions would be. But they are a very important political support for Soviet policy, since they bring to power regimes that are not a part of the Western camp.

The West, and especially Great Britain, have now to pay for past mistakes. They often supported the reactionary upper-class regimes in Asia and Africa. The result is that now, whenever such a regime is overthrown, the new rulers will take an anti-British and often an anti-Western attitude. Naturally, the Soviet Union exploits this fact to her own advantage by playing the role of the anti-colonialist power for which it has the ideological tools. As I shall try to show later, it does not, however, insist that the new powers become integrated into the Soviet bloc and is satisfied with their neutrality. The encouraging trend in the Kennedy administration is that it also tends to accept neutrality as a satisfactory stance; there is no doubt that the United States has more of a historical tradition behind the ideas of anti-colonialism and national independence than the Soviet Union.

CHAPTER FOUR

The meaning and function of Communist ideology

The question that raises perhaps the greatest difficulty of all for the realistic understanding of the nature of Soviet Russia and her political intentions is that of the meaning of Communist ideology. If it is true, as I have tried to show, that Russia since 1923 has not been a revolutionary system, has not attempted to bring about revolutions in the Western countries, and, in fact, has tried to contain them, how is one to look upon the fact that the Russians constantly speak of "the final victory of communism in the world," and of capitalism as the enemy which eventually will be displaced by communism, etc.?

To understand this apparent paradox, one must understand *ideologies*.[1]

"An ideology" is a system of ideas. In talking, for instance, about conservative ideology one refers to the conservative system of thought, etc. This use of ideology may be called descriptive. Since the middle of the nineteenth century one finds other, more dynamic concepts. The *dynamic* concept of ideology, which I use here, is based on the recognition of the fact that man has longings and passions that are deeply rooted in his nature and in the very conditions of human existence.[2] These

[1] The word was used first by the French philosopher, Comte Antoine Destutt de Tracy (1754–1836).

[2] For a detailed discussion of the needs inherent in hu-

inherently human needs are freedom, equality, happiness, and love. If these needs remain unsatisfied, they become perverted into irrational passions like the striving for submission, power, destruction, and so on. In many cultures these irrational passions are the main driving forces, yet only few societies openly admit that they want destruction or conquest. Man's need to believe that he is prompted by human and constructive impulses is so great that it always makes him disguise (to himself and to others) his most immoral and irrational impulses, making them appear as though they were noble and good.

In the history of the last four thousand years the great spiritual leaders of mankind—Lao-tse, Buddha, Isaiah, Zoroaster, Jesus, and many others—have articulated the deepest longings of man. It is remarkable how similar are the fundamental ideas that have been expressed by these various leaders. They penetrated the crust of custom, indifference, and fear by which most people protect themselves from authentic experience, and found followers who awakened from half-slumber to follow them in their ideas. This happened in China, India, Egypt, Palestine, Persia, Greece—where new religions and philosophical schools were formed. But after a while these ideas lost their strength. While people in the first flush of bloom *experienced* what they thought, they slowly began to have purely cerebral, alienated thoughts, *instead* of authentic experiences.

This is not the place to discuss the complex and difficult problem of why this deterioration occurs. It suffices to say that it would be much too easy to explain the

---

man nature, cf. E. Fromm, *The Sane Society*, Rinehart & Co., Inc., New York, 1955, also *Man for Himself*, Rhinehart & Co., Inc., New York, 1947.

problem by the fact of the death of the charismatic leader. It is even not enough to point to the fact that freedom, love, and equality are qualities for the achievement of which one needs courage, will, and the capacity for making sacrifices; nor is it enough to say that much as people want freedom, they are also afraid of it, and want to escape from it, and hence that when the first period of enthusiasm has evaporated, people are no longer capable of holding on to the original ideas. True as all this may be, there is another and more important reason. Man, in the process of history, changes his environment and changes himself. But this process is slow. Aside from primitive societies, the development of civilization and the development of man has proceeded in such a way that the majority of men have had to serve the minority, because the material basis for a dignified life for all was not available. How could the ideal of love and of equality be experienced authentically over any length of time by slaves, by serfs, by the poor whose lives were mainly a struggle against starvation and sickness? How could the ideal of freedom remain alive among those who had to submit to the demands of the few who had power over them? Yet people could not live without faith in these ideals, and without the hope that in time they could be realized. The priests and kings who came after the prophets made use of this need. They appropriated the ideals, systematized them, transformed them into a ritual, and used them to control and to manipulate the majority. Thus the *ideal* was transformed into an *ideology*. The words remain the same, yet they have become rituals, and are no longer living words. The idea becomes alienated; it ceases to be the living, authentic experience of man, and becomes instead an idol outside of him, which he worships, to which he submits, and which he also uses in order to cover up and rationalize his most irrational and immoral acts.

The ideology serves to bind people together, and to make them submit to those who administer the proper use of the ideological ritual; it serves to rationalize and to justify all irrationality and immorality that exist within a society. At the same time the ideology, containing in itself the frozen idea, as it were, satisfies the adherents of the system; they believe themselves to be in touch with the most fundamental needs of man, with love, freedom, equality, brotherliness—because they hear and say these words. And at the same time, however, the ideology also *preserves* these ideas. While they become rituals they nevertheless remain expressed; they can become living ideas again when the historical situation enables man to awaken and to experience again as real that which had become an idol. When the ideology ceases to be a ritual, when it becomes connected again with individual and social reality, then it is retransformed from ideology into an idea. It is as if the ideology were a seed, resting for years in sand and then transplanted into fertile ground where it grows again. An ideology, then, is at the same time a deceptive *substitute* for an idea and its *preservation*, until the time has come for its revival.

Ideologies are *administered* by bureaucracies that control their meaning. They develop systems, they decide what is right and what is wrong thinking, who is faithful and who is a heretic; in short, the manipulation of ideologies becomes one of the most important means for the control of people through the control of their thoughts. The ideologies become systematized and acquire their own logic; words have their specific meaning and—this is very important—new or even opposite ideas are still expressed in the terms of the older ideological frame of reference. (One of the most drastic examples of this is Spinoza's negation of the God of monotheism which he expressed in terms of a definition of God apparently only slightly different from the orthodox definition.)

The ideas of Marx were transformed into ideologies. A new bureaucracy took over, and established its rulership on principles exactly the opposite of the original ideas. The Russians say that they are a classless society, that they have achieved a true democracy, that they are moving toward the withering away of the state, that their aim is the fullest development of the individual personality, the self-determination of man. These are Marx's ideas; indeed, they are ideas that Marx shared with other socialist and anarchist thinkers, with enlightenment thought, and, in the last analysis, with the whole tradition of Western humanism. Yet, the Russians have transformed these ideas into an ideology; a bureaucracy which makes the state increasingly powerful at the expense of the individual, rules in the name of the ideas of individuality and equality.

How can this phenomenon be understood? Are the Soviet leaders plain liars deceiving their people? Are they cynics who do not believe a word they say?

This is a puzzling question; many people are prone to assume that the Russians either fully mean what they say, or that they are outright liars. Yet if we were to examine ourselves more carefully, we might find that we too do the same thing without being aware of it. Most people in the West believe in God, hence in God's principles of love, charity, justice, truth, humility, etc. Yet these ideas have little influence on our behavior. Most of us are motivated by the wish for greater material comfort, security, and prestige. While people *believe* in God, they are not *concerned* with God, that is, they do not worry or lose sleep over religious or spiritual problems.[3] Yet we pride ourselves on being "God-fearing" and call the Russians "godless." Or, most Americans believe that the capitalist system under which we live is based on the free, unmanaged market, on private property, a minimum of government control, on individual initiative. While that was true one hundred years ago, it is not true now. The means of production are essentially not controlled by those (still only a small minority) who own them; individual initiative is drowned in a bureaucratic system and more often found in "Western" films than in real life; the "free" market has become a directed and manipulated market; the state, instead of interfering minimally, is the biggest employer and customer and supports industry whenever it seems desirable to the "government-business-armed services" bureaucracy. We say that we are an alliance of freedom-loving people, yet quite a number of dictatorships belong to our alliance. We accuse the Communists of wanting to proselytize us and make communism a world system—but we say that "it is our aspiration also to see the Russian people freed from their present enslavement, and the Chinese people too. We want people everywhere to be free."[4] Are *we* all liars? Are *they* all liars? Or are we, and they, genuinely stating convictions?

[3] Cf. S. A. Stouffer's illuminating study on Civil Liberty. He finds that in a nation-wide sample, a vast majority believes in God, while very few are worried about religious or spiritual problems; the majority are worried about problems of money, health, and education. (*Communism, Conformity, Civil Liberties,* Doubleday & Co., Inc., Garden City, N.Y. 1955.)

[4] Thomas K. Finletter, *Foreign Policy, The Next Place,* Frederick A. Praeger, New York, 1960, p. 65, cf. l.c. p. 58.

In order to fully understand that these alternatives are not the only ones, it is useful to think of one of the most important discoveries of Freud: the nature of *rationalization*. Before Freud, it was generally believed that unless a person were lying his conscious thoughts are what he *really* thinks. Freud discovered that a person can be fully sincere, subjectively, and yet that his thought may have little weight or reality, that it may be only a cover, a "rationalization" for the real impulse which motivates him. Examples of this mechanism are known to many people by now. Who does not know the scrupulously moral person who in the name of virtue and goodness dominates his wife and children and deprives them of their freedom and spontaneity? He is not lying when he recites his principles, yet if we analyze him, that is to say, if we study his effective motivations, we find that a wish for power or control or even a sadistic impulse to strangle any kind of spontaneity is what in reality motivates him. This reality is unconscious—while his consciousness is not real. Yet he is sincere and, in fact, would be genuinely indignant if his motives were even questioned. Moreover, his ideology is not simply an empty lie and a means to dominate his family all the better because he uses noble phrases and thus impresses them. He actually has a genuine longing for goodness, virtue, and love, but, instead of acting upon these impulses, he transforms them into words and deceives himself with the illusion that he is in touch with love when he talks about love.

Stalin or Khrushchev, using the words of Marx use them *ideologically*, just as most of us use the words of the Bible, of Jefferson, of Emerson, ideologically. We fail, however, to recognize the ideological and ritualistic character of Communist utterances, just as we overlook the ideological and ritualistic character of many of our own statements. Hence, when we hear Khrushchev pronounce Marx's or Lenin's words, we believe that he means what they meant, while the fact is that these ideas are no more real to him than the wish to save pagan souls was to the European colonialists. Paradoxically, *the only people who take the Communist ideology seriously are we in the United States,* while the Russian leaders have the greatest trouble in shoring it up with nationalism, moral teaching, and increased material satisfactions.

The fact that the Communist ideology is losing its influence on the minds of people in general, and of the young generation in particular, becomes apparent in a number of reports from the Soviet Union. A very vivid description of this development is to be found in a recent article by Marvin L. Kalb, "Russian Youth Asks Some Questions."[5] The author reports from Moscow about a new questionnaire of the "Public Opinion Institute" of *Komsomol Pravda,* organ of the 18-million member Communist youth organization. The paper found it necessary to ask questions like "Do you personally have a goal in life?", "What is it?", etc., not so much for the purposes of a statistical inquiry, but in order to combat the widespread phenomena of apathy and materialism, which are found in the young generation. This is the text of one letter, which is characteristic of others: "'Are you satisfied with your generation?' the questionnaire asked. 'No!' the nihilist answered.

"'Why?' the questionnaire asked. 'I'm 19 years old,' she explained, 'and I am filled with apathy and indifference to everything around me—so much so that grown-ups are surprised and wonder, "So young, and yet so bored; what will happen to her when she is 30?"'

[5] *The New York Times Magazine,* April 23, 1961.

But this should not be surprising, for it is a simple fact: life is just not very interesting. And this view is not only my own, but all those people with whom I am friendly.'"

"'Have you a goal in life?' the questionnaire asked.

"'Earlier, when I still poorly understood life,' she wrote, 'I had a goal—to study. I finished high school; and now I am in an institute part time. But now all my pure dreams lead to only one thing—money.

"'Money is everything. Luxury, prosperity, love and happiness—if you have money, you can have all of these things, and more. . . . I still do not know how I am going to get these things; but every girl dreams about a successful marriage with lots of money. Naturally, not everyone succeeds, for there are more people who want money than who have it. . . . But I assure you I shall succeed. My conviction is based on the fact that I always do what I want; and what I want I normally get.'"

I do not mean to imply, of course, that this letter is representative of all the young generation in the Soviet Union. But the survey and the publication of letters like this show how seriously the leaders take the problem.

We in the West, of course, should not be surprised. We are dealing with the same problems of juvenile delinquency and juvenile immorality, and for the same reasons. The materialism, prevalent in our system as well as in the Soviet Union, corrodes the sense of meaning of life in the young generation and leads to cynicism. Neither religion, humanist teaching, nor Marxist ideology is a sufficiently strong antidote—unless fundamental changes occur in the whole society.

Just because ideology is not synonymous with lies, just because they—and we—are not aware of the reality behind the conscious ideology, we can not expect that they will—or could—tell us in an aside "we really don't mean what we say; all this is for public consumption, for keeping control over the minds of the people." Maybe there is an occasional cynic who thinks this; but it is the very nature of ideology that it deceives not only others, but also those who use it. Hence the only way of recognizing what is real and what is ideology is through the analysis of actions and not in accepting words for facts. If I watch a father treating his boy harshly because he considers it his duty to teach him virtue, I shall not be so foolish as to ask the father for his motivations; instead I shall examine his whole personality, many other acts of his, many of his nonverbal manifestations, and I shall arrive at an evaluation of the weight of his conscious intention in comparison with his real motivation.

To return to the Soviet Union, what is its ideology? It is Marxism in its crudest form; the development of man is bound up with the development of productive forces. With the development of productive forces, techniques, modes of production, man develops his own faculties, but he also develops classes which become increasingly antagonistic to each other. The development of new productive forces is hampered by the older social organization and class structure. When this contradiction becomes sufficiently drastic the older social organization is changed to accommodate the full development of the productive forces. The evolution of mankind is a progressive one; both man and his domination of nature develop increasingly. Capitalism is the most highly developed system of economic and social organization, but the private ownership of the means of production throttles the full development of the productive forces and thus hinders the full satisfac-

tion of the needs of all men. Socialism, the nationalization of the means of production plus planning, frees
the economy from its shackles; it frees man, it abol-
ishes classes and eventually the state. At present a
strong state is still needed to defend socialism against
attack from abroad, but the Soviet Union is already a
classless, socialist society. Capitalism, still beset with its
inherent contradictions, must one day adopt the socialist system, partly because of its incapacity to cope with
its own contradictions, partly because the example of
the socialist countries will be so compelling that all
countries will want to emulate it. Eventually, then, the
whole world will be socialist, and this will be the basis
for peace and the full realization of man.

This is, in short, the Soviet catechism. It contains a
mixture of ideology and theory.

First a word about the *theory*. There is one difficulty
the Western observer must overcome. We are not surprised that medieval thinking was structured in the
frame of reference of theology. History was seen in
terms of God's creation, man's fall, Christ's death and
resurrection, and the final drama of the second coming
of Christ. Controversies, and even purely political disputes, were expressed in terms of this central frame of
reference. The eighteenth and nineteenth centuries
had a secular political-philosophical frame of reference. Monarchy versus republic, liberty versus submission, environmental influence versus innate human
traits, etc., were the battlefields.

We in the West still think in a frame of reference
that is partly religious, partly political-philosophical.
The Russians, on the other hand, have adopted a new
frame of reference, that of a socio-economic theory of
history, which, according to them, is Marxism. The
whole world is looked upon from this perspective, and

argument and attacks are expressed in terms of it. For the Western observer for whom such theories are at best the business of a few professors, it is difficult to understand that the Russians constantly talk in terms of class struggle, conflicts within capitalism, victory of communism. The Westerner assumes that this talk must express an aggressive and active attempt to proselytize the world. It may be useful to remember that our religious ideology, in which, for instance, Christians believe that all men will eventually believe in the true God, etc., does not imply that we are all set to convert the pagans. It is simply that, considering our central frame of reference, we have to express our ideas in certain terms; the Russians, having their frame of reference, do so in others.

As I indicated before, Soviet thinking is evolutionary and sees as the central factor in human evolution the development of the productive forces, the transformation of one social system to the next higher one. This view is not ideological in the sense in which I have used the term, but is the way the Soviet leaders really look at history, following in a crude form Marx's historical theory. It is ideological only in the negative sense that the Soviet leaders do not employ this theory to analyze their own system. (Such a Marxist analysis of the Soviet system would immediately show the fictitious character of Soviet ideology.) For most Western observers, however, the theory lends itself to serious misunderstanding. When the Communist catechism says, "Communism will be victorious all over the world," or when Khrushchev said "We will bury you," these statements should be understood in terms of their historical theory that the next stage of evolution will be that of communism, but that does not imply that the Soviet Union sees it as its task to bring about this change by force, subversion, etc.

It is important to understand the ambiguity of the Marxian theory. It is a theory that claims that historical changes occur when the economic development permits and necessitates the change. This aspect of the theory is one that was the basis of socialist reformist thinking in Europe, as represented by Bernstein and others. These socialists believed in the "final victory" of socialism, but they postulated that the working class need not—and could not—push events. They held that capitalism had to go through all the necessary stages, and eventually, at some unspecified time in the future, it would transform itself into socialism. Marx's view was not as deterministic and passive as that. Although he too thought that socialism could be ushered in only when the economic conditions were ripe for it, he believed that at this point the working class and the socialist parties, who by then would be in the majority, would have to take an active part in defending the new system against all hostile attacks from the former ruling groups. Lenin's position deviated from Marx's in that he substituted the avant-garde for the working class, and that he had more faith in the efficacy of force, especially in a Russia which had not yet gone through its bourgeois revolution. The point I want to emphasize is that the Marxist goal of the final victory of socialism was common both to the nonactivist reformists and to Lenin. The formula itself—"Final victory of communism"—is a historical prediction and perfectly applicable to an evolutionary, nonaggressive policy as represented by Khrushchev.

In judging whether Khrushchev aims at a "world revolution" it would be useful to ask oneself what one means by "revolution." Of course, the word can be used in many different meanings, the most general one being that of any kind of complete and violent change of an existing government. In this case, Hitler, Mussolini, and Franco were revolutionaries. But if one uses the concept in a more specific sense, namely the overthrow of an existing, oppressive government by popular forces, then none of these three men could be called "revolutionaries." In fact, this usage is generally accepted in the West. When we speak of the English, the French, the American revolutions, we refer to revolutions from below, and not from above; to the popular attack against authoritarian systems not to the seizure of power by an authoritarian system.

It was in this sense that Marx and Engels used the term revolution, and it was in this sense that Lenin believed he had started his revolution. He was convinced that the avant-garde expressed the will and the interests of the vast majority of the population, even though the system he created ceased to be the expression of popular will. But the Communist "victories" in Poland, Hungary, etc., were not "revolutions" they were Russian military take-overs. Neither Stalin nor Khrushchev are revolutionaries; they are leaders of conservative, bureaucratic systems, the very existence of which is based on unquestioning respect for authority.

It is naïve not to see the connection between the authoritarian-hierarchical character of a system and the fact that the leaders of such a system can not be "revolutionaries." Neither Disraeli nor Bismarck were revolutionaries although they brought about considerable changes in Europe, and remarkable advantages for their respective countries; nor was Napoleon a revolutionary, even though he used the ideology of the French Revolution. But even though Khrushchev is not a revolutionary, his belief in the superiority of communism is perfectly sincere. For him, and probably also for the average Russian, communism and socialism are not, as for Marx, a humanist system which *transcends* capitalism, but an economic system that produces more effectively, that avoids economic crises, unemployment, etc., and hence is more capable, in the long run, of satisfying the needs of a mass and machine society. This is exactly why the Russian Communists believe that peaceful competition between the two systems will eventually lead to the acceptance of the Communist system throughout the world. Their concepts, here as in so many other respects, are those of capitalism—competition in the sphere of economic efficiency. Yet we hesitate to accept Khrushchev's challenge to compete with his system, and we prefer to believe that he wants to conquer us by force or subversion.

Returning to the ideological-ritualistic part of the Soviet cathechism, a few more points must be stressed. In any system which substitutes ritualized ideology for reality, adherence to the correct ideology becomes a proof of loyalty. Since the Russians have ritualized their ideas, they must insist on the "sacredness" or, as they put it, on the "correctness" of their ideological formulae; and, since Khrushchev's authority is based on the legitimacy of his succession to an idolized Marx-Lenin image, they must insist on the unbroken continuity of the ideology from Marx to Khrushchev. As a result there is endless repetition of the "correct" formula, and all new ideas can be expressed only by slight changes of words or emphasis *within* the framework of the ideology. This method is well known to historians of religion. Changes that have made great differences have been expressed only in small alterations within the doctrine, hardly noticeable to the outsider. To mention a more specific example: the official doctrine of the Roman Catholic Church that states that Protestantism is a heresy has never been formally abolished since the sixteenth century. Yet nobody would conclude from this fact that the Catholic Church wants to attack or to forcibly convert the Protestants. Turning away from its attitude in the religious wars of the seventeenth century, the Catholic Church has adopted the attitude of co-existence—yet without changing the official doctrine. As we saw in the last presidential election campaign, only a few bigoted groups were afraid that the election of a Catholic President would mean an attempt by the Vatican to subvert the United States.

This ritualization of the ideology leads not only to the fact that its wording remains sacrosanct, but also that it is used for the direction of men's souls and minds. The difference between religious dogma and Communist ideology lies in the fact that theological statements are the substance of the former, while the latter has its substance in what once was a sociological or historical theory. However, for the purposes of mass influence, the political ideology needs to have moral overtones like "good," "bad," "sacred," and "condemned." In Soviet ideology "capitalism" or "imperialism" are symbols for the powers of darkness, "communism" is a symbol for the powers of light and the quasi-religious aspect is to paint the picture of a cosmic fight between the two powers, the battle of Ormudz and Ariman, of Christ and the anti-Christ. We in the West give a similar twist to *our* ideology, which is just the reverse of the Russian. *We* represent the good, and *they* represent the evil. In fact if we examine all the accusations and the self-praise on both sides, they are remarkably alike in content and also in fervor.

To sum up: The Soviet Union is a conservative state managerialism using Communist-revolutionary ideology. What matters for the evaluation of its foreign policy is its social and political structure, however, and not its ideology. The Khrushchev regime is—and must be —most interested in the development of its system; the bureaucracy ruling in the Soviet Union is expanding and securing the good life for themselves, their children, and eventually for the rest of the population. Khrushchev neither believes in the possibilities for revolution in the West, nor does he want it; nor does he need it for the development of his system. What he needs is peace, a reduction in the armaments burden, and unquestioned control over his system.

Our main distortion lies in the fact that we manufacture a *blend between a revolutionary Lenin and an imperialist Czar, and then mistake Khrushchev's rather conventional and limited movements for signs of the "Communist-imperialist drive for world domination."*[6]

[6] In an important book on foreign policy by W. W. Rostow, *The United States in the World Arena* (Harper & Bros., New York, 1960), the author arrives at conclusions which, in certain respects, are parallel to my own. Rostow points out that "in examining . . . the relations between the present cast of Soviet external and domestic policy in the light of the longer-run forces operating upon it, the criterion is not whether communism as a name will be abandoned; it is not whether, full blown, a parliamentary two-party system of government will promptly emerge; it is rather, whether the linked policies of external expansion, of abnormal repression of consumption and centralized police state rule will be significantly and progressively altered" (p. 418). The author places here the emphasis on

the reality of the social and economic development, rather than on ideology. However, he seems to think that external expansion, police state rule and repression of consumption are essential elements in communism, hence difficult to change; while I believe they were essential for the Stalinist period and not for Khrushchevism.

Nevertheless Rostow expresses considerable hope; "for, the dynamics of Russian history is pressing Soviet society away from the conditions of Communist rule and in the direction of those required for an abandonment by Moscow of its aggressive stance towards the rest of the world" (pp. 422–23). He continues a little later: ". . . but there is every reason to believe that, as the younger men shaped by the war and postwar years come to power, they will be drawn further along the paths leading Russian society to higher levels of welfare and consumption and to greater decentralization and diminished arbitrariness in the exercise of political power. They will find it more congenial to build policy around the interests and capacities of the Russian national state than around the old Marxist-Leninist concepts and Stalin's operational formulae, the relevance and vitality of which have steadily diminished" (p. 426). I believe that Professor Rostow is still too impressed by communist ideology and mistaken in his assumption that a radical shift to more consumption "would create difficult problems for the maintenance of the political and social base of Communist rule in Russia." On the contrary, as I have tried to suggest in the text, full consumption will enable the system to abolish most of its overtly repressive measures, and to proclaim that it is fulfilling the 'socialist' promises for the good life. Why should a population, "caught up in the automobile age" be a threat to the system? More likely it will give solid support to its state managerial bureaucracy, which is making good on some of its promises.

CHAPTER FIVE

The Chinese problem

The future historian may decide that the most outstanding event in the twentieth century was the Chinese revolution. This revolution marks the reversal of a historical trend of several hundred years. China, as well as the other countries in Asia and Africa, had been dominated politically and economically by the powerful European countries; now, not only is China seeking "great power" status, but she is building her own industrial system—although at the price of the violation of human individuality and of severe material sacrifices forced upon her peasant masses.

The Chinese revolution has such historical significance because it is, at this moment, the most advanced example of a world-wide movement, namely, the colonial revolution. The underdeveloped nations in Asia, Africa, and Latin America—the "new world" of the twentieth century—have in common a formula that, in its simplest form, is: nationalism (political independence) plus industrialization. The desire for rapid industrialization is to a large extent, of course, economically motivated, but not entirely. It has its psychological components; industrialization has for such a long time been the privilege of the Western countries—their badge of power—that industrial autonomy has become a goal for the colonial nations for psychological reasons, too.

Historically speaking, the Chinese revolution marks the end of Western colonialism and the beginning of industrialization throughout the rest of the world. While the *aim* of China is shared by most underdeveloped countries, the decisive historical question is whether the Chinese *methods* will eventually also be adopted by the rest of the underdeveloped world.

A feature of vital historical significance is a Chinese "discovery" that constitutes a real threat to the values of the humanistic tradition. This is the discovery that a poor country with insufficient material capital can use another form of capital, namely its "human capital" by centrally organizing and directing the physical energy, the passions and the thoughts of all its inhabitants.[1] This totally organized human "raw material" can replace a good proportion of the material resources that are lacking. To be sure, there have been examples of the attempt to mobilize and direct the physical energy and the thought of people before, in history. This is the way the Egyptian pyramids were built; it is how the Nazi armies marched, and the Russian workers produced. Yet none of these previous attempts have

[1] This point has been expressed most clearly by A. Doak Barnett in his *Communist China and Asia* published for the Council on Foreign Relations by Harper & Bros., New York, 1960. [Aside from Barnett's book, among the most important writings about China used in this chapter are: Benjamin I. Schwartz, *Chinese Communism and the Rise of Mao*, Harvard University Press, Cambridge, 1952. John K. Fairbank, *The United States and China*, Harvard University Press, new ed., Cambridge, 1958, Guy Wint, *Common Sense about China*, The Macmillan Co., New York, 1960. In addition, numerous articles in *Foreign Affairs*, and *The China Quarterly*, some of which are quoted in the text.]

reached the degree of thoroughness and totality the Chinese leaders attempt to achieve. Furthermore, so far the Chinese system seems to have succeeded to an unheard-of degree in producing the feeling, even the conviction, in a considerable number of their people, perhaps the majority, that they are making all their sacrifices voluntarily—and even gladly.

How the Chinese succeeded in bringing about this result is a question about which historians will still argue for many years to come. Yet it is already possible to distinguish some aspects of this method. First, they use the Marxist ideology, as they understand it, as an intellectual frame of reference. This gives them a doctrine, or rather, a dogma that provides a core to which all thoughts and plans can be referred. This dogma leaves no doubts. And it is backed up by the mythical figures of Marx, Engels, Lenin, and by the idolized Mao Tse-tung, and by the fact of the success achieved by the Soviet Union. This "theoretical" aspect of the Chinese system fits in with a past in which knowledge was the most valued property and the key to advancement in the bureaucratic system that governed China for a thousand years before the 1911 revolution. The Communist leaders are the new mandarins; they know the "book," and they prove their power by referring to the book.

However, new elements have been added to the Mandarin and Confucian tradition. They are a peculiar mixture of religious fervor, Russian methods of obtaining confessions and self-accusations, and the most advanced psychological method of persuasion. The quasi-religious motivation in itself is complex. To put it in a simple formula, the Chinese say: Every person is a product of his environment and can be changed if the environment is changed. Those who can not be changed must be eliminated.[2]

The first part of this formula represents eighteenth-century enlightenment philosophy, a theory according to which the environment is the only factor which accounts for character differences, attitudes, virtues, and vices. Mixed with this enlightenment formula is a concept that is similar to the thought of the Catholic Church. While most men can be saved by the Church (in the Chinese formula by the salutary influence of the new environment), those who can not be converted are lost. What is distinct about the Chinese method compared to other forms of dictatorships and communism is that it does not *primarily* rely on force, but on persuasion, and furthermore that this persuasion is not only intellectual, but to a large extent emotional—based on the person's sense of guilt, isolation, and his wish to be reunited with the group—now the party and the community, and no longer the family as it was in the past.

This does not mean that force is absent; it has its place within the process of persuasion. There are fundamental differences between this and the Stalinist method. Stalin wanted to liquidate all dangerous elements, and the Chinese want to "educate" them. Never did the Russians make such an all-out attempt to mold the minds and passions of men as have the Chinese; never has a psychological method of "persuasion" (individual and social brain-washing) been more universal, as thorough, and—as it seems—as successful.

[2]Cf. Jerome Ch ên, Writers and Artists Confer., *The China Quarterly*, October–December 1960, p. 76 ff. and Benjamin Schwartz, Totalitarian Consolidation and the Chinese Model, *The China Quarterly*, January–March 1960, p. 18 ff.

The Chinese problem

The particular feature of Chinese communism is, if one puts it in a nutshell, that the Chinese leaders have recreated an effective religion. To be sure, one without a god—but, after all, neither Taoism nor Confucianism had a theistic concept of God in their systems. This new religion is centered around a strict morality, which in itself should not seem strange to any Westerner. Pride, conceit, selfishness are considered to be the main vices; they must be replaced by humility and unselfish service to the nation. This new religion has many ramifications. It affects the person's political views, his personal habits, his philosophy. In every sphere of life there is a "right" and a "wrong," a "good" and an "evil." By "thought reform," education and re-education, the individual is made to see the "evil" within himself—and is taught how to achieve the "good"; he is taught to lose his "impurity" and to acquire "purity." Thoughts and feelings which deflect from this politico-moral goal are evil and must be struggled against with all might.[3]

This "totalist" system is as effective and drastic as it can be found anywhere; it is opposed to all those values of individualism and free critical thought, which are some of the most precious flowers of Western culture. It must be noted, however, that it is somewhat naïve to forget that such thought control was customary in many religions and this kind of indoctrination has existed in many cultures throughout the world.

These and other characteristics of Chinese communism, however, can be properly understood only if we look at Chinese communism as a whole, and then compare it with the Soviet Russian system.

[3] An excellent description of this process is to be found in Robert J. Lifton, *Thought Reform and the Psychology of Totalism*, W. W. Norton, New York, 1961.

What is characteristic, first of all, of the Chinese revolution, is the fact that it is primarily a peasant revolution, and not a workers' revolution. It has been often remarked that this very fact alone shows that it is not a revolution in the Marxist sense. The Chinese leaders had a tough job to find the theoretical formula to bridge this obvious contradiction, and there is no need here to follow the fine points of their argument.[4] The revolution followed an increasing course of collectivization in the agrarian sector, which in 1958 culminated in the constitution of the Communes.

In order to appreciate China's agricultural problem one has to consider the fact that while the United States has 570,000 square miles of land under cultivation, with a population of 180,000,000, China has only 425,000 square miles of cultivated land with a population of about 650 to 700 millions.[5] However, while there is little prospect of increasing this area to any considerable extent, there is a possibility, as Fairbank points out[6] of increasing the production of food by means of irrigation and fertilization, which would add minerals to the soil. (One must note here what could be done if part of America's surplus food, for the storage of which we pay more than the cost of our entire economic aid for Asia, could be given to China on terms of cheap and long-term credits.)

Aside from the insufficient arable land, China suffers from her primitive agricultural techniques. This can be seen most clearly from the following figures: in

[4] Cf. the extended argument on the question of a specific Maoist line between B. Schwartz and K. Wittvogel in *The China Quarterly*.

[5] These figures are taken from John K. Fairbank, l.c. p. 17.

[6] l.c. p. 19.

the United States it takes 1.2 man-days to cultivate and harvest an acre of wheat, while in China it takes 26 man-days.[7] It seems that in the first Five Year Plan, collectivization did not do more than increase the annual output by 2.65 per cent, which is little more than the population increase of 2.2 per cent.[8] (The official Chinese statistics claim an annual growth of 3.7 per cent in output.) The relative smallness of China's agricultural base is still more aggravated by the fact that China exports a considerable amount of foodstuffs to pay for her industrialization. This results in a very poor diet for her peasants. However, there seems to be reason to assume that China can obtain a much better food supply for her peasants once her industrial output permits her to produce tractors, fertilizers, and irrigation facilities, and to buy foodstuffs from other parts of the world, especially from Southeast Asia.

Having this in view the Chinese government has put the whole emphasis on the industrialization of the country. So far, the results of the process of industrialization are quite impressive, even if one does not fully accept the Chinese official figures. A recent Western estimate of China's gross national product for 1950–57 "made by William W. Hollister who made use of official raw data together with independent calculations, gives an annual rate of growth of 8.6 per cent with 1952 as the base and 7.4 per cent with 1953 as the base."[9]

[7] Fairbank, l.c. p. 26.

[8] Cho-Ming Li, Economic Development, The First Decade, Part II, *The China Quarterly*, January–March 1960.

[9] Cho-Ming Li, l.c. p. 36, quoting W. W. Hollister, *China's Gross National Product a Social Account 1950–1957*, The Free Press, Glencoe, Ill., 1958, p. 2.

These figures, which are also accepted by Barnett, are all the more impressive if one compares them with the rate of growth in other Asiatic countries, especially India, which started her first Five Year Plan under conditions not too dissimilar from those of China. The Indian rate of growth from 1950–51 to 1955–56 (the first Five Year Plan) was only 3.3 per cent (or 4 per cent, according to other sources[10]) that is, one half (or less) of the Chinese rate.[11] It hardly needs to be emphasized that, if this development continues in the same fashion, the Chinese example will prove to be so attractive for India and other underdeveloped countries that their populations may become willing to pay the price of regimentation and loss of freedom in exchange for economic improvement, hope, and the satisfaction of national pride. It is interesting to compare the Chinese and the Indian figures with those of Japan, which had an annual rate of growth of her gross national product of 4.6 per cent during the period 1898–1914, 4.9 per cent from 1914 to 1936, while her real national income is estimated to have increased during 1956–59 by an average annual rate of 8.6 per cent.[12] As Barnett quite rightly remarks: "The performance of the Japanese indicates that it is possible for a non-Communist country to make rapid economic progress without resorting to totalitarian methods, but Japan is no longer

[10] Wilfred Malenbaum, "India and China, Contrasts in Development Performance," *American Economic Review,* vol. 49, June 1959, pp. 284–309 quoted by A. D. Barnett, l.c. p. 45.

[11] Cf. Cho-Ming Li, l.c. p. 37, also for the following figures on Japan.

[12] Based on Table VI–I p. 45 in Jerome B. Cohen, Japan's Postwar Economy, Indiana University Press, Bloomington, 1958, quoted by Barnett, l.c. p. 45.

an underdeveloped country, and it is in comparison
with other underdeveloped nations in Asia that Communist China's rate of growth takes on a particular
significance."[13]

Closely related to China's industrial progress is, of
course, the growth of her military strength. Needless
to say that China is not lacking in manpower,[14] and
for that matter, in a disciplined one, instilled with national pride and fanaticism. But in addition China can
increasingly produce her own military equipment. Estimates are of course quite unreliable on this score, but
China will be able to manufacture her own atomic and
thermonuclear weapons within at most a very few
years.

The most important point for American foreign policy is, not only to understand the nature of the Chinese
Communist regime, but to appreciate its differences
with Russia and the conflicts between the two regimes
which follow from these differences. Until not so long
ago Soviet Russia and Communist China were treated
as if they were twins. (This kind of approach is still
to be found in the press and in many utterances of the
less informed politicians.)

What is deceptive about the relations between the
Soviet Union and China is the fact that they have the
same ideological system and a political alliance. For
those who can not see the differences between ideologies and facts, this means that the two systems are
more or less identical. The truth is, however, that the

[13] A. D. Barnett, l.c. p. 45.

[14] China, aside from her regular army, is also developing
a militia which might grow to a strength of 120 million men
and women with some basic military training. Cf. Ralph
L. Powell, "Everyone a Soldier," *Foreign Affairs*, Oct. 1960.

reality of the two systems is radically different in spite of their ideological similarity.

The Soviet Union has changed from a revolutionary workers' and peasants' state to a politically conservative industrial managerialism. Soviet Russia is the last of the great European states arriving at full industrialization, and is in the process of becoming one of the richest and most powerful "have" states in the world. Its ideology is still that of revolution, Marxism, etc., but this ideology is increasingly wearing thin, as far as its effective influence on the minds and hearts of people is concerned. The ideology of a society with equality, brotherliness, and classlessness, of the withering away of the state, is more and more in contrast to the reality of a society built along rigid class differences.

Communist China, as of today, is one of the "have-not" nations; like other underdeveloped countries, the Chinese population has a standard of living twenty or more times below that of the industrialized countries. The Chinese have been exploited and treated with contempt by the Europeans for over a hundred years. (It is not without significance that Stalin, too, had great contempt for the Chinese.) Now they are awakening under the leadership of gifted, resolute, and uncorrupt men, the very same men who started and won the revolution. They are nationalistic, proud, and sensitive to any kind of slight from the West. They have decided to transform China into a powerful industrialized state, and to become one of the leading powers in the world. There is (so far) little corruption.

The Chinese leaders have a concept of communism which is in radical opposition to that of Marx. While his system of communism aimed at the emancipation and the full unfolding of the individual, the Chinese Communists attempt the complete collectivization of individuals in order to make them indistinguishable members of a collective; they suppress individuality for the sake of society. Consequently they believe that their system of "communes," in which the vast majority of all Chinese are already organized, is a step toward the realization of communism. They are creating a new form of religion, a peculiar mixture of enlightenment ideology blended with the cultivation and exploitation of guilt and shame. Different as their system is from anything Marx meant by socialism (or by communism), it is equally different from the Russian industrial managerialism. It is only slightly exaggerated to say that the Chinese, the "blue ants" as they are often called in Russia, appear to be as foreign and "wild" to the Russians today as the Russians appeared to the West in 1917 to 1920.[15]

Even though Soviet Russia and China were and still are allied by their common antagonism to the West, and by their common ideology, there is an increasing schism between the two powers. This conflict rests upon several factors. The most important one is probably the fact that Russia is today part of the rich status quo world of the West, and China is part of the poor sector comprising the peoples of Asia, Africa, and Latin America. This is a conflict of a very different nature than the one between Russia and the West. The latter is a battle between two blocs which have much more in common economically than Russia has with China; China, in her effort to become the leader of the colonial revolution, to bring communism to India, Indonesia, the Middle East, and Latin America, is as much or more of a potential threat to the Soviet Union than

[15] Cf. G. F. Hudson, "Mao, Marx and Moscow," *Foreign Affairs*, July 1959: "the analogy is not with Khrushchev's Russia but with the Russia of the late twenties" (p. 565).

to the United States. If China wanted new territory for her ever-increasing population, thinly populated Siberia would be more tempting than the densely populated part of Southern and Southeastern Asia.

In addition to the potential threat as the leader of the colonial revolution, the Chinese leadership constitutes another threat to the Soviet Union's position as the leader of the Communist world. The Chinese Communists, since coming to power, have stated that their own revolution is a "classic example" and the model for other revolutions in Asia and all other underdeveloped countries. Since they started the commune system, the Chinese leaders claim that the Russians are behind them on the road to a Communist society. China today is a poor society striving for industrialization with tremendous force; Russia is becoming a rich society trying to develop and to preserve what she has.

The history of the relationship between China and Russia has gone through many phases, which we do not have to discuss in detail. Since 1920–21, when the hopes for a revolution in Europe were fading, the hope for revolutions in Asia became an important point on the agenda of communism. Even then there existed a conflict within the ranks of communism. Lenin thought in terms of support for, and alliance with, the national revolution of the Chinese bourgeoisie against the Western powers, while the Indian, Roy, emphasized the necessity for a workers' and peasants' revolution against their own bourgeoisie.[16]

What is important to remember is that the victory

[16] Cf. the detailed description in E. H. Carr, *The Bolshevik Revolution 1917–1923*, The Macmillan Co., New York, 1953, Vol. III, p. 254 ff. Also the discussion between K. Wittvogel and B. Schwartz in *The China Quarterly*.

of the Chinese Communists was almost entirely a Chinese accomplishment, with almost no help from Russia. Stalin supported the Kuomintang, Chiang Kai-shek's government, and there is good reason to assume that the very weakness of the Kuomintang regime suited him well.[17] This is borne out by the fact that in the Yalta agreement Stalin succeeded in re-establishing Russia's rights in Manchuria, and after the war he pressed the Kuomintang to surrender its former sovereignty over Outer Mongolia.

When the Kuomintang government had to relinquish Nanking, Stalin instructed the Soviet ambassador to accompany the Chiang Kai-shek government to Canton, while most of the other ambassadors remained in Nanking to await the Communists. Even after the success of the Chinese Communists, economic help from Russia was quite limited. Chinese investments were virtually all made with internal savings, while financial assistance from the Soviet Union was not substantial.[18] From 1950 to 1956 the Soviet Union promised technical and financial aid to 211 projects. The financial aid consisted of loans and not grants; it was enough only to pay for about one third of the equipment needed for the Russian-sponsored projects, and during 1952 to 1957 the amount of Russian credit available for new investment constituted merely 3 per cent of the total state investments.[19]

[17] Cf. G. Wint, l.c. p. 96 and for the whole problem of Chinese-Russian relations, Boorman, Eckstein, Mosley, Schwartz, *Moscow-Peking Axis*, Publ. for the Council of Foreign Relations by Harper & Bros., New York, 1957.

[18] Cf. Cho-Ming Li, l.c. pp. 38–39 and A. D. Barnett, l.c. pp. 47–48. Cf. also Louis Fischer, *Russia, America and the World*, Harper & Bros., New York, 1960, Chapter IV.

[19] These figures are quoted from Cho-Ming Li, l.c. pp. 38–39.

This limited financial aid, nevertheless, does not alter the fact that the technical assistance that the Russians gave by sending specialists was of great importance, and the first Five Year Plan could hardly have been accomplished without such aid. However, even as far as technical assistance is concerned, one must not forget that Chou En-lai wrote in the *People's Daily* in October 1959, that the "Soviet Union has sent over 10,-800 experts to the East European satellites, over 1500 to China during the previous decade,"[20] and furthermore that most Russian experts left China in 1960.

The ambiguity of Russian-Chinese relations developed into a manifest antagonism only since 1959, although all the elements of the conflict existed and were occasionally mentioned before. The main point of contention between the two forces is: the question 1) of peaceful coexistence with the West, 2) of peaceful methods to achieve the victory of communism in various countries, 3) of atomic armament for China, and 4) of whether the Russian or the Chinese way is the more correct path to communism.[21]

[20] Quoted by Cho-Ming Li, l.c. pp. 38–39.
[21] Cf. aside from works already quoted, Zbigniew K. Brzezinski, Patterns and Limits of the Sino-Soviet Dispute, *Problems of Communism*, September–October, 1960, pp. 1–7, Donald S. Zagoria, Strains in the Sino-Soviet Alliance, *Problems of Communism*, May–June, 1960, pp. 1–11, G. F. Hudson, "Mao, Marx and Moscow," *Foreign Affairs*, July 1959, pp. 561–72, "Peking on Coexistence," *Foreign Affairs*, July 1960, pp. 676–87, A. M. Halpern, Communist China and Peaceful Coexistence, *The China Quarterly*, July–Sept. 1960, pp. 16–31. Furthermore H. Boorman et al., Moscow-Peking Axis (which was written before the important change in 1958), quoted before, and Frank N. Trager, *Marxism in South East Asia*, Stanford University Press, Stanford, 1959. Cf. also the interesting article by Sidney

The main question from the standpoint of Western foreign policy, undoubtedly, is the conflict between the Russian position in favor of coexistence, and the Chinese policy which is less hesitant to risk the possibility of war. This conflict seems to have broken out during Khrushchev's visit to Peking on the tenth anniversary of the Chinese revolution in 1959, if we accept A. M. Halpern's convincing analysis.

While the speeches during the celebration emphasized peaceful coexistence, Khrushchev left Peking without even signing the usual friendly communiqué together with Mao. What had happened? "We must assume," says Halpern, "that Khrushchev, on arrival in Peking, notified the Chinese leaders that he was satisfied that a mutual accommodation with the West was both desirable and attainable and that he intended to enter into serious negotiations. He probably dictated to them some limits on their future military development. He almost certainly demanded at least a modified style of behavior in foreign affairs, and more likely some substantive policy changes. He probably also assured them that he would not negotiate away their interests, but at the same time urged them to be prepared for less than their maximum demands."[22]

After some meditation, it seems that the Chinese agreed that their method of dealing with South and Southeast Asia had not been successful, but with regard to the policy toward the West (and the other problems mentioned above) their attitude hardened

Lens on the Russo-Chinese rift in the Communist parties in Real Story Behind India's Border Dispute with China, pub. in the Chicago *Daily News,* Dec. 9, 1959.

[22] A. M. Halpern, l.c. p. 26. Cf. the somewhat different version in Richard Lowenthal's Diplomacy and Revolution: The Dialectics of a Dispute, *The China Quarterly,* January —March 1961, p. 186.

increasingly. They adopted the thesis of an inevitable and permanent conflict between the two camps, and they took the position that American "peace gestures" were nothing but a smoke screen for the United States wish for world domination. The Russian position on the other hand, remained clearly one of "peaceful co-existence." The following statements represent the two positions quite succinctly: *Khrushchev:* "Let us not approach the matter commercially and figure out the losses this or the other side would sustain. *War would be a calamity for all the peoples of the world.*"

"Imagine what will happen when bombs begin to explode over cities. These bombs will not distinguish between Communists and non-Communists . . . No, everything alive can be wiped out in the conflagration of nuclear explosions."

"Only an unreasonable person can be fearless of war in our day."[23]

On the other hand, this is the Chinese position, according to Mao Tse-tung: "If the imperialists insist on unleashing another war, we should not be afraid of it . . . World War I was followed by the birth of the Soviet Union with a population of 200 million. World War II was followed by the emergence of the socialist camp with a combined population of 900 million. If the imperialists insist on launching a third world war, it is certain that several hundred million more will turn to socialism."[24]

[23] Respectively from Khrushchev's speeches before the Indian Parliament, February 11, 1960, to members of the French Peace Council, March 23, 1960, and in Vladivostok, October 8, 1960, quoted by Donald S. Zagoria, l.c. p. 3 (my italics, E.F.).

[24] Yu Chao-li, *Red Flag*, March 30, 1960, quoted by Zagoria, l.c. p. 3. Cf. also the article in *Red Flag*, April 15th

Considering the difference between the Russian and the Chinese attitudes toward war and peace, two questions arise. First, whether these differences are as real as they appear to be or whether, as some people are prepared to believe, Khrushchev was using his "soft" line only in order to create a favorable climate for the summit meeting. Considering the prolonged and intense ideological argument going on between the two blocs, an argument that was resolved by a compromise solution (after three weeks of negotiations) almost completely in favor of Khrushchev's position in the declaration of the 81 Communist Parties in Moscow, 1960, it does not make sense to assume that the Chinese would put up all this violent ideological opposition if they knew or assumed that Khrushchev was making a point only for short term tactical reasons. To answer that the whole Chinese opposition is only part of a fine plot which wants to make it appear *as if* Khrushchev is serious is no longer realistic political analysis, but paranoid thinking.

The other question is why the Chinese take such a stand on thermonuclear war, of which they seem to be much less afraid than are the Russians. One obvious reason has often been mentioned. With their lack of centralization and their much larger population, they may think that thermonuclear war would bring to their system a much smaller degree of destruction than would be the case for the Soviet Union or the United States, and hence leave them the strongest power in a postwar world. Whatever their views on this topic are, one must not forget that the Chinese leaders have an evangelistic fervor, which the Russians lack for rea-

issue which takes the same line, quoted in "Peking and Coexistence," *Foreign Affairs,* July 1960, pp. 676–87.

sons that were discussed earlier. However, whether these considerations mean that the Chinese want war and that their course is, under all circumstances, an unchangeably aggressive one, is another question to which we shall return in a little while.

On the question of peaceful methods in the fight for communism, the difference between the Russians and the Chinese is as strong as it is in the question of co-existence. An article cited above (from *Red Flag*, April 15, 1960) says that the emancipation of the workers and peasants, "can come about only by the roar of revolution and certainly not by the roar of reformism." The Yugoslav leaders, for whom the ritualistic word "revisionists" is employed, are singled out as the arch enemy and the center of world revisionism. But they often serve only as a foil for the real opponent, Khrushchev, who of course can not openly be called a revisionist. Yet Khrushchev's position becomes quite clear in the declaration of the 81 Communist Parties quoted before, with its emphasis on peaceful, economic competition between the two systems, as against revolutionary activities.[25]

Actually, the conflict between the Russian and the Chinese lines is by no means restricted to the problems of the industrial countries (where it is largely theoretical and unreal). It is very acute with regard to the policy toward various underdeveloped countries. It is quite likely that the sudden cessation of the Communist offensive in Iraq in the summer of 1959 was due to Khrushchev's pressure and against the intentions of the Chinese; the more clear-cut case is that of Algeria. In his report to the Supreme Soviet, in October 1959, Khrushchev, reversing his previous stand against de

[25] See pages 95 to 96.

Gaulle's plans, suddenly came out in favor of a North American cease-fire plan, while the Chinese have continued to label de Gaulle's plan as "nothing but a trick from A to Z."[26]

Eventually, the Chinese-Russian conflict centers on the leadership within the Communist movement. The Chinese leaders claim that their communes are a decisive step forward in the direction of true communism, and that Mao Tse-tung is the leading theoretician of the Communist camp, while the Russians naturally deny this claim.[27] This conflict is by no means just a matter of personal jealousy. It touches upon the very important question of whether the Soviet Union or Communist China will eventually be the leader of all underdeveloped countries and, specifically, of the Communist Parties within these countries. The difference between Russian and Chinese communism is a very real one. While Russia represents a conservative industrial managerialism, she has to support the colonial revolutions for the sake of her own world political position, always qualified by the concern for her own security and the possibility of an arrangement with the Western bloc. China, on the other hand, with ideas contrary to those of Marx's socialism, has developed, thus far, an evangelical faith in an egalitarian type of mass society; this faith is based on a zealous expectation that the

[26] Quoted from D. S. Zagoria, l.c. p. 8. Cf. also his whole discussion of this point from which I draw.

[27] This discrepancy is expressed, for instance, in formulations like these: On the occasion of Mao's birthday in 1958 Khrushchev congratulated him on his *"faithfulness* to the great ideas of Marxism and Leninism," while a Chinese broadcast asserted that "we must study Marxism-Leninism *as well as* the Mao Tse-tung ideology"—implying that the latter comes first. (Quoted from D. S. Zagoria, l.c. pp. 3–4.)

communes constitute a short-cut to the new form of society and a deep disbelief that capitalism can change its intention to destroy the Communist countries.

The Russian-Chinese antagonism is apparent not only in the conflicts regarding views on coexistence, on peaceful transition to socialism, etc., but in many practical questions of foreign policy. In addition to the difference in attitude toward de Gaulle and, probably, to Iraq, it is well known that Khrushchev expressed his regrets at the aggressive attitude of the Chinese in the Chinese-Indian border conflict. There is also serious competition going on between Russia and China, not only in various Communist parties all over the world, but especially in such strategic places as the Congo, Algeria, and Cuba, where the Chinese are trying to win over the local leaders to their more aggressive policies while the Russians are in the position of having to exercise a moderating influence and at the same time talking sufficiently "tough" in order not to lose the battle for influence to the Chinese competition.

More important, perhaps, is the Russian wish not to equip the Chinese with atomic weapons if they can help it. There is a good deal of evidence of Chinese pressure being exerted on the Soviet Union to grant nuclear weapons to China, and a Russian reluctance to comply with this wish.[28] There has been joint East German[29] and Chinese pressure for atomic armament in case the Western powers place thermonuclear weapons at the disposal of West Germany. Khrushchev, on the other hand, in an undated letter to the European Federation against Atomic Armament, made public by the Tass News Agency on March 18, 1959, stressed the

[28] Cf. the discussion by D. S. Zagoria, l.c. pp. 9–10.

[29] East Germany, aside from Albania, is the Communist system which is friendly to Peking, yet is being forced to follow the Moscow line.

"undesirability of expansion of the so-called atomic club," and warned that United States action to supply nuclear weapons to her allies would set off "a kind of chain reaction in the dissemination of nuclear weapons all over the world."[30]

One problem must still be considered now, because it is of fundamental importance for any consideration of the future of Chinese policy. The problem is whether the aggressiveness of China's political position at present indicates that China is bent on territorial expansion, and hence eventually on war.

Considering her population pressure and the low productivity of her agriculture, one might argue that for economic reasons China needs to seek territorial expansion. Such expansion could take place either in the direction of the thinly populated Outer Mongolia and Siberia, or in the direction of the heavily populated Southeast Asia with its fabulous resources of rice, oil, rubber, etc. While an increasingly aggressive China may one day take such a course of territorial expansion, there are many reasons why this is not the method which the Chinese leaders would prefer. Expansion toward Siberia would make the Soviet Union the enemy of China, and bring about an anti-Chinese, United States-Soviet Union coalition, which would be a mortal danger for China. As to expansion toward the southeast, which could occur only with Russian implicit or explicit support, there is no real economic *need* for such expansion. It is true that China needs many of the raw materials obtainable in Southeast Asia, but the problem, for her, is not primarily that of *owning* the countries that have oil, rubber, etc., but of having free and unhindered trade with them at fair prices.

[30] Quoted from D. S. Zagoria, l.c. p. 10.

The crucial point in China's whole economic situation is the fact that China has almost no long-term credits, and is being forced to industrialize on a shoestring, that is to say, by forced saving at the expense of general consumption. This is the picture given by Barnett. "As China embarked on its second Five Year Plan," he says, "it appeared, therefore, to be proceeding almost completely on a pay-as-you-go basis, and this may have been an important factor behind the radical changes in domestic policies which Peking introduced during 1957–1958. The dramatic decisions to set up decentralized, small-scale, labor-intensive industries, to mobilize labor on a mass scale for irrigation and other projects requiring little capital investment, and to regiment China's population and resources further by establishing the communes may all be related, in some respects at least, to the fact that by 1958 Communist China was carrying out its development programs without long-term foreign loans."[31]

In spite of their fervor in pursuing their type of communism, their intense nationalism, their pride, and their aggressive language, there is no reason to assume that the present leaders of China are not realistic and rational men who prefer to see their efforts succeed peacefully, rather than to provoke a war, even though they are less anxious to avoid such a war than the Russians are. This is also Barnett's conclusion: "There are many reasons to believe, however, that in their broad strategy Peking's leaders do not think primarily in terms either of Chinese territorial conquest abroad or of exporting revolution by overt Chinese aggression. World conquest in traditional military terms and world revolution in Communist terms are very different concepts.

[31] A. D. Barnett, l.c. p. 231.

Yet, Peking does attach high priority to the building up of its military strength, and in many ways it can attempt to use pressure and force while still trying to avoid a major war."[32] Even after the recent stand of the Chinese leaders against the Khrushchev coexistence policy, Barnett does not believe that the Chinese have really given up their aim of avoiding war and of competitive coexistence which they followed before the fiasco of the "1000 flowers period." "One cannot," says Barnett, "of course, rule out completely the possibility that Peking has made a major decision to place an increased reliance on military force to achieve its goals. However, as of the early autumn of 1959, there is little to indicate that the Chinese Communists have, in fact, decided to pursue a general policy of large-scale military aggression. The new pressures they have been exerting on China's neighbors have to date been limited pressures, and apparently Peking's aims both in regard to the Sino-Indian border and Laos have also been limited.[33] In both of these situations, in fact, local factors rather than broad tactical considerations seem to provide the main explanation for Peking's recent actions, and it appears likely that after attempting to make local gains, Peking will probably try once again to re-emphasize the carrot rather than the stick in its relations with South and Southeast Asia."[34]

If one takes a sober view of the Chinese situation and is not blinded by passionate hatred of their kind of

[32] A. D. Barnett, l.c. p. 76.

[33] As far as Laos is concerned, it seems likely that this is much more a Russian than a Chinese concern; in fact, it is not too farfetched to assume that the Russians are engaged in Laos in order to prevent it from falling into Chinese hands. (E.F.)

[34] Barnett, l.c. pp. 108–9.

communism, one might arrive at this conclusion: the more difficult, economically, the Chinese position is, the more intolerant will the regime in China become, and the more aggressive its foreign policy. If the present policy of maximal economic isolation and of political humiliation of China is continued, the aggressive tendencies within China will increase and help Khrushchev's enemies within the Soviet Union to gain victory. This course is likely to lead to the thermonuclear arming of China, hence of Germany, and eventually to the brink of war. If, on the other hand, the Peking government is given credits and the possibility of free trade, and its seat in the United Nations, and if the fulfillment of the country's economic needs is not threatened by hostile governments in Southeast Asia, there is a very reasonable chance that China will revert to its earlier policy of competitive coexistence which was in effect until 1958.

CHAPTER SIX

The German problem

There are many political problems which stand in the way of an American-Russian understanding: Korea, Formosa, Laos, the Middle East, the Congo, Cuba, South America. Yet there is probably no problem which forms a greater obstacle to understanding than that of *Germany*.

When the Second World War ended there was agreement that Germany must be prevented from ever again becoming a military menace to either the West or to Russia. While the fantastic Morgenthau plan for making her a mainly agricultural state was rejected, it was agreed that Germany was not to have a strong army. The Germans themselves also seemed to agree to this. Adenauer spoke out firmly against the idea of a strong German military force, and the Social Democrats, the strongest opposition party, were violently opposed to armament and *"Atomtod"* (atom-death). There were also big popular demonstrations against atomic armament in several German cities.

Now, not too many years later, the situation has been completely reversed. Germany is already the strongest military power in Europe, with the exception of Russia. Her generals (all of whom served under Hitler) insist that Germany needs atomic weapons for her self-defense; the Social Democrats, especially since Willy Brandt took over the leadership of the party, are hardly less ardent promoters of German military might than the Adenauer party.

The Western position is simple enough; the Soviet Union in her wish to dominate the world (as demonstrated by her conquest of the East European states after the war) will overrun Western Europe unless Europe can be defended by sufficiently strong military forces.[1] Without an armed Germany, however, Europe is not strong enough to resist a Russian onslaught, hence a rearmed, militarily strong Germany is needed to defend the free world. This argument is further strengthened by the assumption that present-day Germany is democratic and peace-loving, and thus can not possibly be a threat to Russia or to anyone who does not have evil intentions.

The Russians, on the other hand, have never shared this viewpoint; they feel menaced by a militarily strong West Germany, and they believe that a rearmed Germany will repeat the Kaiser's and Hitler's attempts to conquer Russia.

Is the Western emphasis on the peace-loving and democratic nature of the present German regime sufficiently convincing to dispel the Russian fears? Is Germany as "changed" as the Western allies proclaim?

Germany is the latest of the big industrial European

[1] This strategic idea is in contradiction to the "massive retaliation" strategy under President Eisenhower, which meant that our atomic strength would deter Russia from invading Europe. At this moment it seems that the Kennedy administration has shifted European strategy from atomic retaliation to the build-up of conventional forces which would, of course, make the military role of Germany still more important than under Eisenhower. Cf. Maxwell D. Taylor, "Security Will Not Wait," l.c., and Henry H. Kissinger, l.c.

powers (with the exception of Russia) to arrive at full maturity. The world had already been divided among the older powers (England, France, Holland, Belgium). Germany, whose industrial development assumed an extraordinarily fast pace after 1870, had a highly developed industry (characterized, like that of Japan, by a great degree of cartelization) and a disciplined and capable labor force, yet it was geographically a relatively small country lacking raw materials and markets to absorb its industrial potential. At the same time, Germany (especially Prussia) had a feudal class, which had developed a most remarkable military cast. It was competent, devoted, and extremely nationalistic. The blending of industrial expansion with her military potential led Germany on to the path of war. At the beginning of the twentieth century, Germany tried to challenge England's naval supremacy by her own naval program.[2]

Already in 1891, with the foundation of the "Alldeutscher Verband," the slogan of the "Volk ohne Raum" ("People without Space") began to spread. Hugenberg, one of the representatives of German industry and later the leader of the conservative party who helped Hitler to gain power, was one of the co-founders of this organization. The Austro-Hungarian provocation in 1914 permitted the war-minded armed forces, allied with the German heavy industry, to put enough pressure on the more peacefully minded but weak civilian government under Bethmann-Hollweg to enforce the decision for war. During the war the political spokes-

[2] The deterioration of German-British relations was not due, as is often believed, to the German plans for economic penetration of Turkey (the Bagdad Railroad), but to her navy program by which she threatened England.

men of German heavy industry, the Alldeutscher Verband, as well as the newly organized Vaterlandspartei and also the traditional parties from the right of the center party to the conservatives, supported the old expansionistic war aims, which in memorandum form had been presented to the Reichschancellor by the Zentralverband Deutscher Industrieller (Central organization of German industrialists), on May 20, 1915. General Ludendorff, the real leader of the German war machine, in a memorandum, (September 14, 1916) approved more or less of the same aims: territorial expansion in the East, expansion in the West at the expense of France, Holland, and Belgium for the support of the German heavy industry.

These groups prevented a peace in 1917, and thus were responsible for the final German defeat.

The Kaiser had been only the puppet of the industrial and military forces, which unleashed the war. After the Kaiser had gone, and after a short revolutionary period that threatened the very existence of these industrial and military forces, they reasserted themselves within the framework of the democratic Weimar Republic. The army was modernized and rebuilt (secretly, and against the stipulations of the Versailles Treaty) and industry flourished and its leaders (or their political spokesmen) achieved an ever-increasing political role in the Weimar Republic. After 1929, however, radicalism began to assert itself. The Communist and Socialist Parties were counting on adding the millions of unemployed as supporters and thus gaining a majority in the Reichstag.

At this moment Adolf Hitler offered his services. He promised two things: First, to destroy the Communist and Socialist Parties and thus to save industry from the danger of losing its predominant position; second, to create such a nationalistic frenzy that the basis for full and open rearmament, and eventually a new bid for a "place under the sun," would be attained.

There is ample material by now to show how Hitler was supported by German heavy industry and how he could never have seized power without this support. On February 20, 1933, Hitler met twenty-five of the leading German industrialists (including Krupp) and repeated more or less the program he had presented on January 27, 1932, to a smaller group: the protection of private enterprise, an authoritarian regime, and rearmament, which would be decided on not in Geneva but in Germany as soon as the inner enemy had been eliminated. To the generals he made a speech in 1933 (February 3) in which he demanded living space in the East, together with the conquest of new markets for exports.

Hitler's program was not essentially different from that of the industry-army coalition of the First World War, and it was supported by the same groups.[3] Neither the industrialists nor the generals liked Hitler, but he seemed to be the only man who could try again where the Kaiser had failed. His mad racism was the necessary price to pay for his services.

The important thing is that it was not Hitler who caused World War II, but the same alliance between industry and the military which had been the driving

[3] For this whole period, from the first to the second World Wars, cf. *Der Nationalsozialismus-Dokumente 1933–45*, ed. W. Hossbach, Fischerbücherei 1957; W. Thyssen, *I Paid Hitler*, New York, 1941; George W. F. Hallgarten, *Hitler, Reichswehr und Industrie*, Europäische Verlagsanstalt, Frankfurt/Main. Franz L. Neumann, Behemoth, New York, 1942. Erich Fromm, *Escape from Freedom*, Rinehart & Co., Inc., New York, 1941.

force behind World War I. (The fact that the generals were more cautious in their planning than Hitler and that some of them turned against him does not alter this basic constellation.) Again, as in the First World War, the German élite made a severe mistake in the choice of their leader. The parallel between Ludendorff and Hitler is, indeed, striking. Both were gifted yet hysterical, half-mad nationalists with unbridled imaginations; both failed to recognize the point at which there was no longer any possibility of winning the war. One difference, and an important one, is that Ludendorff, when he eventually saw that everything was lost, gave up, while Hitler, the more insane and destructive of the two, was determined to have all of Germany destroyed together with him in a grandiose *Götterdämmerung*.

The Germans lost, and once more the industrialists and the militarists disappeared in the background. The occupation by the Western allies did not lead to a fundamental social and political change. The Nazis were considered the true culprits rather than the people who had hired them. While in 1918, in spite of the clamor for it, one had not hung the Kaiser, one did hang his successors, the top leaders of Nazism. This act, however, can be likened to exorcising the devil. The logic being that since the Nazis had been responsible for the war, and since they had been thoroughly destroyed, Germany now under her new leadership was a democratic, peaceful state. When after 1947 the tension with the Soviet Union increased, the West was more and more prone to urge the old enemy to rearm and thus to prove by implication that Hitler had not been so wrong in his thesis that it was Germany's function to save the "Christian culture of the West" from the "barbaric hordes of Bolshevism."

The new Germany has not only the industrial and military potential for a new aggressive role, but also the nationalistic potential which can be used for aggressive plans. First, the German government has never recognized the Oder–Neisse line as a final border. While the wisdom and justice of the decision to give undisputably German parts of Eastern Germany to Russia and Poland and to deport millions of Germans from these territories can be seriously questioned, this decision is a fact, concurred in by the Western allies although not in a formal peace treaty.

Actually, the results of this step were much less harmful, economically and socially, than one might have feared. These provinces were among the poorest of Germany, and their population, which emigrated to Western Germany, has been so successfully absorbed into the booming German economy that probably only very few would want to return to their homeland now, even if they could. This, however, does not alter their clamor for the "stolen territories," and no German political party dares to curb this clamor. (Not even that of the former Sudetendeutsche who shout for the return of *their* land, actually stolen by Hitler from Czechoslovakia.)

This nationalistic feeling is kept alive and it can be fanned to great intensity any day a German government should want to do so. Its potential is no less than that of Danzig, the Corridor, Austria, and the Sudetenland on which Hitler built his war preparations. While the German government could show its peaceful intentions by recognizing the Oder–Neisse line the statement that Germany will not try to recover her former territory *by force* is a meaningless phrase (in the style of many of Hitler's declarations) since it is quite obvious that they could recover these territories in no other way than by force.

Developments in Germany are particularly ominous if one examines the trend of the last five years. This trend is not toward democratization and peace, but toward a new ascendancy of the militarists and of nationalism. The Bundeswehr has already shed many of the democratic trimmings that were supposed to demonstrate its difference from the old Prussian militaristic spirit. The generals have already taken the unconstitutional step of demanding publicly atomic arms for the defense of the country. They are also demanding an increased German navy; they are negotiating with Franco for bases in Spain, etc., etc.

Many former Nazis are still in high government positions. (Dr. Globke, a high civil servant under Hitler and author of the most important commentary on Hitler's racial laws, is chief of Adenauer's chancellory office.) It is characteristic that one of the main attacks against Willy Brandt, the Social Democratic opponent of Adenauer, is the argument that he emigrated from Germany under Hitler, and thus was not a loyal patriot.

Germany is gaining a new ascendancy in Western Europe, this time not by war, but by her economic superiority in a unified Western European economic bloc. Such a Germany, dominating France, Holland, Belgium, and perhaps Italy, would be much stronger than she ever was before. It is not surprising that the Russians are suspicious of this development and feel threatened by it. It is surprising that Great Britain and the United States seem to have no suspicions; in both countries the fear of Russia has eliminated the fear of a new powerful Germany which could turn against the West just as well as against the East.

CHAPTER SEVEN

Suggestions for peace

What are the various answers given to the question of how to solve the present-day world conflict without resorting to nuclear war?

1) PEACE BY DETERRENT; ARMAMENTS AND ALLIANCES

The first and still the most popular answer in the United States runs like this: the Communist camp is motivated by the wish for world domination, hence there can be no real end to the cold war. But nuclear war can be avoided if the United States has such a retaliatory capacity ("second strike" capacity) that it would deter the Russians from attacking us.[1] Hence our freedom, as well as peace, depends on sufficient nuclear armament, plus military alliances so that the Soviet leaders will be deterred from attacking us. As

[1] For example, Oskar Morgenstern, one of the most distinguished of the military analysts writes: "The fact that the United States has not been attacked (directly) by Russia since the end of World War II is due either to the possibility that Russia did not want to attack us (even if our deterrent force had been much smaller or perhaps even zero) or to the strength of our deterrent force, presumably in particular to our nuclear capability. We can forget about the first possibility; we would have been attacked had we been much weaker." *The Question of National Defense*, Random House, New York, 1959, p. 29.

Henry A. Kissinger, a very influential expert writes: "With no advantage to be gained by striking first and no disadvantage to be suffered by striking second, there will be no motive for either surprise or pre-emptive attack. Mutual invulnerability means mutual deterrence. It is the most stable position from the point of view of preventing all out war."[2]

What do our experts think we should do in the event of a Russian attack against positions outside the United States but to whose defense we are committed? Most strategists, especially those of the Army and Navy, believe we should be prepared to meet political and military challenges with a limited war capability, backed up by a "finite" nuclear deterrent to keep the situation from "escalating" into a total war. Such strategists reject the notion of "massive retaliation" for limited enemy actions as leading to total and mutual destruction, just as they consider the aim of our nuclear force is to *prevent* its ever being used. Among these is General Maxwell D. Taylor, who appears to represent the thinking of the Kennedy administration. He writes:

The program would seem to me to require provision for the following principal elements:

a) An invulnerable, long-range missile force with a second-strike capability, i.e. the ability to inflict crippling damage on an enemy even after absorbing a surprise nuclear attack.

b) Adequate and properly equipped mobile forces to cope with limited war, i.e. conflicts short of general atomic war between the two nuclear power blocs.

c) An effective system of alliances.

d) Procedures for assuring the most effective use of the resources committed to the program.

[2] Cf. H. A. Kissinger, *The Necessity for Choice*, Harper & Bros., New York, 1961, p. 33.

If called upon to justify the need for these elements, the planners could advance the following reasons and explanations:

The purpose of preparations for general atomic war is to assure that no such war will ever be fought. In all probability this purpose can be achieved provided there is an appropriate balance of destructive capability between the two power blocs which will make the deliberate choice of general atomic war unthinkable to either.[3]

However, as we shall see, there are experts—especially those representing the Air Force—who disagree with this view and feel that there are circumstances in which we would and should initiate a nuclear war, for example if we were losing a limited war.

Among the adherents of "security by deterrent" one can distinguish two positions. One, which seems to be accepted by the present administration, holds that if both sides have an efficient and stabilized deterrent, nuclear war is practically impossible. This position is based on the assumption that the destruction brought about by thermonuclear war would be so devastating that no sane government would ever try to use these weapons if it expects its opponent to be strong enough to retaliate after an attack. The second position does not hold this optimistic belief in the "impossibility of war" and in the guaranteed success of deterrence. But its adherents fall into two sharply disparate groups. On the one hand, those who urge complete disarmament because they do not believe that the deterrent will prevent war; on the other hand, those who hold that it is possible to *win* a thermonuclear war. These latter experts argue that such a war need not be as utterly

[3] Maxwell D. Taylor, "Security Will Not Wait," *Foreign Affairs*, January 1961, p. 177.

dreadful as many people fear; that its horror can be diminished to a very "bearable" minimum provided we spend enough money on the proper measures, an efficient shelter system, and ever more efficient thermonuclear weapons. The most effective spokesman for this view is Herman Kahn, with whose views I shall deal in the following pages.[4] Kahn has two reasons for believing that it is foolish to think that the deterrent makes war impossible. The first is that there are times when

[4] Cf. H. Kahn, *Report on a Study of Military Defense,* published by the Rand Corp. Santa Monica, Cal., 1958, *The Arms Race and its Hazards,* Daedalus, Fall 1960, and *On Thermonuclear War,* Princeton University Press, Princeton, New Jersey, 1960. In the latter book which reproduces a series of lectures Kahn has given to influential groups from industry and the military, he writes: "It is the thesis of this lecture that if the proper precautions have been made, it would be possible for us or the Soviets to cope with all the effects of a thermonuclear war, in the sense of saving most people and restoring something close to the prewar standard of living in a relatively short time. But there is no reason to believe this will be true unless both nations investigate the problem more thoroughly than has been done so far, and then take the necessary preparations" (p. 71).

Since the publicity stirred up by Kahn's book, there are reports that senior personnel in the RAND Corporation have written letters to editors around the world, denouncing Kahn's views as "troglodytic" and "apocalyptic." (Cf. E. L. Katzenbach, Jr., "Ideas: A New Defense Industry," *The Reporter,* March 2, 1961.) However, it is worthwhile to ask why this criticism was not made when Kahn was talking to generals and industrialists rather than to the general public. Are the RAND officials worried that Kahn exposes to the public the fact that deterrence does not provide the security that has been claimed for it by every authority from the Pentagon to the leading magazines and newspapers?

going to war might be better than its alternatives, assuming, of course, that one could win. Kahn's second argument is that even if the governments of both sides do not want a war the outbreak of war is still possible.

Kahn persuasively destroys the illusion of a safe deterrent by analyzing the different possibilities of war despite nuclear deterrence. These include:

1. *Accidental War.* The possibilities for accidental war include false alarms reacted to by attack, unauthorized behavior, and true mechanical or human error, the chances of which become greater as the number of weapons increases. Further, it is always possible for one side to misread another's defensive or alerting reactions to false alarms as the beginning of an attack, and in "self-defense" to attack first.

As far as the danger of accidental war is concerned, it must be added that there exist a considerable number of potentially paranoid persons among the "normal" part of the population in whom the tension of prolonged expectation of an attack may lead to the outbreak of manifest paranoia carrying the conviction that he—whoever the person is who could give the alarm or push the button—must save the country by starting an attack. This danger lies particularly in the fact that even the full-fledged paranoiac can be perfectly reasonable in his thinking outside of his delusion, and hence he—and even more so the potential paranoiac—is not easy to discover.

2. *The Rationality of Irrationality.* To explain what he means by this, Kahn quotes a graphic example given by Bertrand Russell. " 'This sport is called "Chicken." It is played by choosing a long straight road with a white line down the middle and starting two very fast cars towards each other from opposite ends. Each car is expected to keep the wheels of one side on the white

line. As they approach each other mutual destruction becomes more and more imminent. If one of them swerves from the white line before the other, the other, as he passes, shouts "Chicken!" and the one who has swerved becomes an object of contempt.' It is clear that if one side really wishes to win this game its best (rational) strategy is to commit itself irrevocably to going ahead. If one can convince the other side that one has done this, then the other side must back down. However, if the other side still refuses to back down after the irrevocable commitment has been made, it would be irrational to carry out the rationally made commitment. Since both sides will be attempting to use this strategy, it is also quite clear that the game may end in a disaster.[5]

"The rationality of irrationality war should be distinguished from the situation in which both sides have incompatible objectives which they are determined to achieve, no matter what the risks: in this case war must result. The rationality of irrationality war corresponds to a situation in which neither side really believes the issue is big enough to go to war over, but both sides are willing to use some partial or total strategy of commitment to force the other side to back down. As a result, they may end up in a war they would not have gone into, if either side had realized ahead of time that the other side would not back down, even under pressure."[6]

3. *War by Calculation* [or miscalculation]. By this Kahn refers to the possibility that "after due study, a nation might decide that going to war would be the least undesirable of its choices,"[7] either in the form of

[5] Kahn, in Daedalus, l.c. p. 756.
[6] l.c. p. 757.
[7] l.c. p. 757.

a preventive war, or a pre-emptive war. The case of the pre-emptive war or "anticipatory retaliation" is not really a decision to attack. One side would strike only because it is convinced that the other side is ready to attack. "This is clearly a situation," says Kahn, "in which each side has nothing to fear but fear, yet the knowledge that the other side is afraid fully justifies that fear. Many things could touch off a reciprocal fear of surprise-attack situation."[8]

4. *Escalation.* Part of the strategy of the general view of deterrence is that it allows limited war to take place without fear that the limits will be violated—since both sides could then destroy each other. However, under the stress of an actual crisis or limited war, accident or miscalculation might at any time trigger a full-scale cataclysm. "This could occur either because the limits of a limited war are not being observed, or because more parties are being drawn into it, or because the issues themselves become fraught with significances that did not initially exist, or because of some unauthorized or accidental behavior by subordinates. It is difficult to supply a plausible reason for escalation, when it is to everybody's interest to control things, yet almost everybody considers that it can and perhaps will happen."[9]

5. *Catalytic War.* By this last possibility, Kahn refers to either an ambitious third nation, or a desperate third nation which might force one of the two main powers who themselves do not want war to make an attack nevertheless. The type of catalytic war which to Kahn is "much more likely and important" than one resulting from the schemes of an ambitious nation may

[8] l.c. p. 760.
[9] l.c. p. 762.

occur when "a desperate third nation thinks it has a problem which can be solved only by war." Kahn says, "Let us imagine a war between India and China which the Indians were losing. The Indians might also feel that if they induced the United States to strike at China and Russia, this would solve their problem, and any method they used to achieve this end was as good as any other. Conversely, let us imagine a situation in which the Chinese felt hard pressed (possibly over Formosa) and told the Russians, 'We are going to strike the United States tomorrow, and you might as well come along with us, for they will undoubtedly strike you, even if you do not do so.' As stated, the situation may seem somewhat implausible, but one can devise hypothetical situations which make it seem more plausible than I have done here. One may wish to broaden the definition of catalytic war. Any method by which a nation uses military or diplomatic power to embroil larger nations or increase the scope of the conflict could be called catalytic. By this definition, World War I was a catalytic war, set off by Serbia and Austria, which also had some overtones of 'reciprocal fear of surprise attack' and 'self-fulfilling prophecy,' because the side which mobilized first was likely to win. It meant that even a defensive mobilization (by the Russians) touched off a defensive-offensive mobilization (by the Germans) in much the same way some believe that a badly designed, quick-reacting force can be touched off by defensive moves by the other side."[10]

The various possibilities mentioned here are all possibilities of war not provoked by the wish or the will of either of the two main power blocs to start an all-

[10] l.c. pp. 763–64.

out nuclear war.[11] Yet it is quite clear that the very situation of two powers prepared to destroy each other, if and when necessary, creates a considerable probability for the decision to start a war by either side, even though both would prefer to avoid it.

The crucial point in these considerations lies in the fact that, once given certain constellations, the most conscientious and rational of military leaders on both sides will be forced to start an attack in spite of the fact that they do not want a war. As Kahn points out, with each "new generation" of weapons, the war nobody wants becomes more terrible in prospect, for the logic of deterrence demands continual build-up to be sure that no matter how many bombs the enemy sends, we will have some left to destroy him. Kahn even goes to the extreme of discussing the possibility that a nation might wish to base its deterrence on a Doomsday Machine which would threaten to blow up the world along with the aggressor. He writes: "Our normal military forces are frightening enough and they are improving rapidly . . . The most spectacular thing about

---

[11] Kahn is not, of course, the only expert who has outlined the dangers of accidental, catalytic war, escalation and miscalculation. Among others, H. Brown and J. Real describe the risks in a manner similar to Kahn's. For example, they write: "Even with only two nuclear powers and four nuclear nations in the world, there is a finite chance that all-out nuclear war could be triggered accidentally. This could be brought about as the result of either mechanical or human failure. No machine is perfect. No human being is free from the possibility of making errors of judgment. Already, for example, there have been several accidents involving American aircraft carrying nuclear bombs." *Community of Fear,* Center for the Study of Democratic Institutions, Santa Barbara, California, 1960, p. 25.

the arms race is that it *is* a race and one that is being run with some celerity."[12]

Considering the sober and conservative assumptions presented by Kahn and confirmed by many other sources, it would seem clear that the expectation that even a stable deterrent protects us from nuclear war is at best a hope or a guess, but by no means the kind of safe prediction which the general public takes it to be.

There have been attempts by experts, especially those representing the Army and Navy to work out weapons systems that would eliminate or hold to a minimum the dangers of accident or miscalculation that Kahn underlines so deftly. These attempts are based on two assumptions. One is that danger of accident or pushing buttons too hastily can be minimized by an "invulnerable" deterrent, one which would survive no matter how strong the first strike might be; therefore there would be no ultimate advantage to surprise attack. The Polaris submarine missile system might serve this purpose, especially if Russia were also to have a similar deterrent. As Oskar Morgenstern describes it, an effective invulnerable deterrent would be composed of atomic submarines and airplanes, which being mobile could not be destroyed by one surprise attack. "If both sides adopt the Oceanic System," he writes, "the most curious consequence is that *both parties gain together:* in making their deterrence effective they protect themselves against accidental war by enabling the opponents to verify signals of attack and to filter out the false ones. Clearly . . . an invulnerable force does not have to rise immediately when a signal of attack, which may be only a false alarm, is

[12] H. Kahn, l.c. p. 764.

accepted as real. Even if the signal is true the retaliation can be spaced out over time giving all the favorable possibilities mentioned earlier."[13]

Note that Morgenstern says "if both sides adopt the oceanic system. . . ." It is imperative for invulnerable deterrence strategy that each side know that the other is depending solely upon weapons designed for this strategy; that is, weapons of great destructiveness but relatively low accuracy, capable of destroying cities but not of pinpointing arms installations and holding undestroyed cities as hostages. If Russia, say, believes that we also have "counterforce" weapons, and therefore the capacity to strike first, they will doubt our professions of purely punitive intent. In situations of tension they may fear that we will take the initiative, and so take it themselves—knowing that we can answer with our invulnerable city-busters but preferring to bank on their civil defense rather than on our good intentions. Thus, if the invulnerable deterrent is to deter, we must give up all accurate first-strike missilery, all intelligence activity that locates enemy missile bases (i.e. the weapons and activities championed by the Air Force), and even hold our invulnerable deterrence capacity *down* to a level where it cannot be used in large masses to make up for its inaccuracy so as to destroy missile bases as well as cities. For example, it is estimated that if we have more than forty-five Polaris submarines we are no longer convincingly incapable of destroying an enemy's second-strike capacity, even with the uncertainties of aiming from a submarine. Is it likely that in the coming all-out arms race we will voluntarily limit ourselves in this manner? And

[13] Oskar Morgenstern, l.c. p. 98.

even if we do, how can we convince the Russians that we have? As Schelling points out, we could not *show* the Russians our military installations to prove that we had only weapons of the "invulnerable" type, because the weapons, to be invulnerable, must have secret locations.

Another assumption necessary for the invulnerable deterrent to work is that both sides act coolly and rationally, always aware of what the other side's power is at any given time, and always waiting in a tense situation in order to make sure. Kissinger describes the necessary conditions of invulnerable deterrence as follows: "Deterrence, to be effective, has four requirements: 1. The implementation of the deterrent threat must be sufficiently credible to preclude its being taken as a bluff. 2. The potential aggressor must understand the decision to resist attack or pressure. 3. The opponent must be rational, i.e., he must respond to his self-interest in a manner which is predictable. 4. In weighing his self-interest, the potential aggressor must reach the conclusions the 'deterrer' is seeking to induce. In other words the *penalties* of aggression must outweigh its benefits."[14] The key concept here is one that assumes rationality on the part of both opponents. The proponents of the invulnerable deterrent must propose this, for where there is the possibility of such destruction, the danger is not worth risking unless one can trust people to act rationally.

How valid are these assumptions? Even if we had an invulnerable deterrent (and *what* an invulnerable deterrent is, always depends on the latest progress in the development of weapons), this would not protect at least half of the American population from being de-

[14] Henry A. Kissinger, l.c. p. 41.

stroyed, provided the enemy is not deterred.[15] Furthermore, even with the invulnerable deterrent, all the possibilities for an unwanted war, as presented by Kahn, remain the same, with only one modification; we would have more time to wait for confirmation of an attack, since there would not be the chance that an attack could seriously cripple our retaliatory capacity. On the other hand, the decentralization of the units of deterrents (submarines, planes in the air, etc.) actually increases the chances of irrational actions.

The invulnerable deterrence theorists are forced to base all their hopes on mutual knowledge and rationality between the United States and Russia. This is in one sense ironic, since these same experts usually deny any possibility of understanding or rational agreement between the United States and Russia when it is a question of disarmament. In fact, if there is any agreement for rational actions, it is exactly the reverse of the argument of the deterrent theorist. In times of peace one might assume that people have sufficient rationality to arrive at solutions which are beneficial for both sides. If this were not the case then, indeed, it is not likely that people would show this rationality of thought when threatened with the immediate extinction of a large part of their population or after even

---

[15] The only safe way of deterring would be to show the Russians our military installations, so that their fear of our retaliatory power does not depend on a guess which can be wrong, but on solid knowledge. As Thomas C. Schelling, (*The Strategy of Conflict*, Harvard University Press, Cambridge, 1960, p. 176) has pointed out, this procedure, while desirable, would at the same time give the opponent such knowledge of the location of our missile bases as to make such a procedure impractical.

"only" one city with several million people has been pulverized.

However this may be, it is the common assumption of most "invulnerable deterrent" strategists that they do not see any alternative to the efficacy of deterrence. If the deterrent would not work then, indeed, the United States would cease to exist. For, as Morgenstern puts it, "Defense against these weapons is practically nonexistent; indeed, it is now impossible. It exists only in the fertile imagination of some men, not in physical reality."[16] In contrast to this view expressed by Morgenstern, is another view represented by Herman Kahn, who claims that the deterrent does not necessarily preclude war, but that thermonuclear war would by no means have to be as catastrophic as the "nuclear pacifists" on the one hand, and atomic strategists like Morgenstern assume. The general thesis which Kahn wants to prove is expressed in the following statement: "Perhaps even more pertinent is this question, 'How happy or normal a life can the survivors and their descendants hope to have?' *Despite a widespread belief to the contrary, objective studies indicate that even though the amount of human tragedy would be greatly increased in the postwar world, the increase would not preclude normal and happy lives for the majority of survivors and their descendants.*"[17]

Kahn considers that it is only squeamishness which keeps experts from facing the possibilities of a total war. "*If we assume that people could survive the long-term effects of radiation, what would the standard of living in their postwar world be like?* Would the survivors live as Americans are accustomed to living—with

[16] Oskar Morgenstern, l.c. p. 10.
[17] H. Kahn, *On Thermonuclear War*, l.c. p. 21.

automobiles, television, ranch houses, freezers, and so on? No one can say, but I believe there is every likelihood that even if we make almost no preparations for recuperation except to buy radiation meters, write and distribute manuals, train some cadres for decontamination and the like, and make some other minimal plans, the country would recover rather rapidly and effectively from the small attack. This strong statement is contrary to the beliefs of many laymen, professional economists, and war planners."[18]

What are the proper preparations which will secure relatively harmless consequences of nuclear war? If the United States had a system of fall-out shelters all over the country, plus a system of blastproof shelters (plus arrangements for rapid entry), plus thirty to sixty minutes of warning, plus strategic evacuation of cities (that is, several days before an attack), the estimated casualties would be "only" 5,000,000 in an attack on one hundred and fifty cities; on the other hand, if none of these preparations were made, Kahn assumes 160,000,-000 casualties. The actual figure between these two extremes will lie according to the degree of preparation. For example, Kahn argues that with nothing else but fall-out shelters plus arrangements for tactical evacuation, losses could be held to 85,000,000 people, given thirty to sixty minutes warning.[19]

What about these figures? In the first place, some of the conditions are completely unrealistic, such as the thirty to sixty minutes' warning, when missiles from submarines or from earth satellites would give practi-

[18] H. Kahn, l.c. p. 74.

[19] H. Kahn, *Report on a Study of Non-Military Defense,* The Rand Corporation, Santa Monica, 1958, p. 11 ff., and *On Thermonuclear War*, pp. 113–14.

cally no warning time and those from Russian bases at most fifteen minutes. In addition, tactical evacuation into blastproof shelters, even if there were a fifteen-minute warning, could only give people enough time to trample one another to death before they entered the shelters. As Morgenstern writes, "If the warning time is in minutes only, as it will be at best, almost no one will reach the few shelters in the large cities if these come under attack."[20] As for any evacuation of cities which was not begun well before the event (and in that case would be provocative of an attack), Morgenstern writes: "It is nonsense . . . to evacuate the Los Angeles area from the sea on across the Sierra would surely take many hours at best, but the warning time for a missile fired from under water, say 100 miles distant, is zero."[21] But even Kahn himself is by no means certain of his estimates. Whether or not all Americans will be destroyed still depends on other factors. "On the other hand," he says, "even with the assumed shelter systems, heavier casualties and more extensive destruction are also conceivable. Unless U.S. active offenses and active defenses can gain control of the military situation after only a few exchanges, an enemy could, by repeated strikes, *reach almost any level of death and destruction he wished.*"[22]

In his *On Thermonuclear War*, Kahn discusses the "pessimistic" assumption that if all fifty-three large metropolitan areas in the United States were completely destroyed, still one-third of the United States population and one-half of United States wealth, being left outside, would be spared. "From this point of view,

[20] O. Morgenstern, l.c. p. 115.

[21] Morgenstern, l.c. p. 121.

[22] H. Kahn, *Report on a Study on Non-Military Defense*, p. 13. (Italics mine, E.F.)

the above destruction does not seem to be a total economic catastrophe. It may *simply* set the nation's productive capacity back a decade or two, plus destroying many 'luxuries'."[23] Kahn, while making these reassuring statements, is always willing to admit that there is also another possibility, without, however, ever dropping his cheerful prospects for nuclear war. Thus, he speaks of limitless destruction of the United States, unless we can win the war militarily. Or, to give another example, he admits that "in the long run, a purely military approach to the security problem can lead to disaster for civilization, and by long run, I mean decades, not centuries."[24]

But there are many other flaws in his reasoning, which ignores a number of essential facts. First, his whole balance sheet of deaths is based on the shelter idea. But it is generally recognized that within a few years there will be bombs many times more destructive than 10- or 20-megaton bombs, and then shelters will be useless, even if we all live underground. He forgets that it is easier to increase the striking power of nuclear weapons than to increase the safety factor of shelters and hardened bases.[25] As Morgenstern puts it in another context (securing bases from attack): "Hardening imposes a greater burden on a country than the burden the opponent has to assume in order to raise his striking power with which to offset the effects of hardening."[26] It follows that despite all the optimistic figures, if the arms race goes on for five years more, we, the Russians, and a large part of the world are threat-

[23] H. Kahn, *Report on a Study on Non-Military Defense*, l.c. p. 77.

[24] H. Kahn, *On Thermonuclear War*, l.c. p. 160.

[25] Cf. O. Morgenstern's statement, l.c. p. 50.

[26] O. Morgenstern, l.c. p. 50.

ened with much higher losses than the Kahn calculations assume, if not with extinction.

Kahn furthermore gives little consideration to the psychological and political problems which could arise if, according to an estimate of his, all big cities, containing one-third of the population and one-half of the wealth of the country, were destroyed within a few days. He cheerfully states that "nations have taken equivalent shocks even without special preparations and have survived with their prewar virtues intact. In past years these shocks were spread over many years; the one we are considering would take place in only a few days. *But for individual psychological effects* (as opposed to organizational and political effects) *this is good, not bad.* While many normal personalities would disintegrate under hardships spread over a period of many years, the habits of a lifetime cannot be changed for most people in a few days. If you have to take it at all, then from the viewpoint of character stability it is better to take this kind of shock in a short time rather than in a long one."[27]

It is truly amazing how Kahn here makes the most questionable statement in the field of psychology and psychopathology without reference to any scientific data, not even to the most obvious obstacle to his theory, that of traumatic neuroses. To a psychologist, it is much more likely that sudden destruction, and the threat of slow death to a large part of the American population or the Russian population or large parts of the world will create such a panic, fury and despair, as could only be compared with the mass psychosis that resulted from the Black Death in the Middle Ages.

This lack of any psychological insight becomes

[27] H. Kahn, *On Thermonuclear War*, l.c. pp. 89–90.

of crucial importance in considering the only practically feasible part of the shelter idea, that of fall-out shelters. Morgenstern points this out very succinctly.

"Duration of the fall-out determines the length of time it is necessary to remain in shelters. These are small and cramped; people will develop claustrophobia, run out of food and water or fall ill. In short, the point may be reached where in despair they prefer to venture outside, only to succumb to radiation sickness, probably to die. One can barely imagine the psychological situations that would arise and the problems the occupants of the shelter would have to solve for themselves. In the minds of the persons in the shelters would be the shattering knowledge of being involved in the greatest disaster the human race has ever seen.

"This would indeed be so: the Black Death, the massacres by the Mongol hordes, or any other large misfortunes either have been spread out over many years, or have involved isolated, widely separated cities, small by modern standards. Here disaster would cover great areas, be *concentrated* in time and still *last* indefinitely, if the enemy so chose."[28]

The traumatic effects of such a catastrophe would lead to a new form of primitive barbarism, the resurgence of the most archaic elements that are still potentialities in every man and of which we have had ample evidence in the terror systems of Hitler and Stalin. It is unlikely that human beings could cherish freedom, respect for life—in short, what we call democracy—after having witnessed and participated in the unlimited cruelty of man against man which thermonuclear war would mean. There is no evading of the fact that brutality has a brutalizing effect on the partici-

[28] O. Morgenstern, l.c. p. 117.

pants, and that total brutality leads to total brutalization. Even in the event of only partial destruction— from sixty to eighty million casualties in America (and corresponding numbers in other countries) one thing is definite: after such an event there will be no democracy left anywhere, only ruthless dictatorships organized by the survivors in a half-destroyed world.

The moral problem is even given less weight in Kahn's reasoning than the psychological one. The only question posed is how many of us will be killed; the moral problem of killing millions of fellow human beings—men, women, children—hardly is mentioned. After wholesale slaughter, the survivors are supposed to live a reasonably happy life. One asks oneself from what kind of moral or psychological position these assumptions are made. One comes to a rather shocking suspicion when one reads the following statement, a quotation from an earlier statement Kahn made in testifying before the subcommittee of the Joint Committee on Atomic Energy on June 26, 1959: "In other words, war is horrible. There is no question about it. *But so is peace.* And it is proper, with the kind of calculations we are making today, to compare the horror of war *and the horror of peace* and see how much worse it is."[29]

I said that this statement is a shocking surprise because one is forced to think that it transcends the limits of sane experience. Anyone who makes such a state-

[29] H. Kahn, l.c. p. 47, footnote (italics mine, E.F.). Answering a reporter who questioned this statement, Kahn said "I meant that the quality of life after a thermonuclear attack would not be much different than before. And who the hell is happy and normal right now? We'd be just about the same after a war—and we'd still be economically useful." (*San Francisco Chronicle*, March 27, 1961.)

ment (or agrees with it) provided he means what he says, must be severely depressed and tired of life; how could he otherwise try to weigh the horrors of thermonuclear war (with, say, sixty million Americans and sixty million Russians killed) with the "horrors of peace"? I believe that the kind of reasoning that Kahn and many others accept is, indeed, understandable only on the basis of personal despair. For people for whom life has no meaning, there is no obstacle to preparing balance sheets of destruction in which they calculate how many dead—between sixty and one hundred and sixty million—are "acceptable." Acceptable to whom? That this kind of thinking has become so popular is one of the gravest symptoms of despair and alienation, and of an attitude in which moral problems have ceased to exist, in which life and death are transformed into a balance-sheet problem, and in which the horrors of war are minimized because peace—and that is life—is felt to be only a little less horrible than death.

We are dealing here with one of the most crucial problems of our age—the transformation of men into numbers on a balance sheet; one thinks it is a "reasonable" calculation to weigh the death of one- to two-thirds of the nation, provided the economy will soon recover. Indeed, there have always been wars; there have always been people who have sacrificed their own lives or killed other humans—out of love of liberty or in mere drunken orgies of hate. What is so new and shocking about the contribution of our age is the cold-blooded use of bookkeeping methods to encompass the destruction of millions of human beings.

Stalin did this with millions of peasants. Hitler did it with millions of Jews. He was motivated by hate, but for many of his subordinates it was simply a bureaucratic measure; regardless of the motive, once the order had been given, millions of human beings were liquidated systematically, economically and totally. Adolf Eichmann is an example of this type of murderous bureaucrat; Robert S. Bird has given a brief yet penetrating sketch of him: "As he has repetitiously unrolled his function," reports Bird from the Eichmann trial in Jerusalem, "in shipping millions of Jews off to extermination camps, he has begun to ring familiar bells in the mind of the courtroom spectator. One suddenly hears speaking the faceless 'company man' of the oversized industrial organization, the alibi-ridden, buckpassing, double-talking, reading-by-ear personality who has been drained of native emotion and principle and filled with an unreal ideology."[30]

All that is said here about the personality of Eichmann can, indeed, as Mr. Bird indicates, be applied to ourselves. Eichmann, he says, has suddenly become more "understandable," a "somewhat encompassable human being." Indeed, Eichmann has become more human, because we can recognize that he is as inhuman as we all are. This new kind of inhumanity, regardless of one's view of Eichmann as an individual, is not cruelty or destructiveness. It is more inhuman than that, although perhaps more innocent, if this were the word. It is the attitude of complete indifference and lack of concern; it is the attitude of total bureaucratization that administers men as if they were things.

It is fashionable today to talk about the inherent evil quality of man, which, allegedly, stamps optimism for a better future as sinful pride. But if we were really so evil, our cruelty would at least be human. But, the bureaucratic indifference toward life, of which Mr. Kahn's graphs and the calculations of others are such drastic

[30] *New York Herald Tribune*, April 23, 1961.

examples, is a symptom of a new and terrible form of inhumanity, one in which man has been transformed into a thing.

These considerations lead us to a further moral point that is often suggested in the debate on disarmament. The alternative is presented as "death or surrender" and the advocates of disarmament are accused of preferring to be slaves, rather than to die. This argument, which proposes armament and the risk of war on *moral grounds*, is misleading in many aspects. Not primarily because the whole alternative is abstract and rather unrealistic politically, but because of the basic moral fallacy which it contains. Indeed, an individual's decision to give his life for the sake of a fellow man's life, or his own integrity and his own convictions, is one of the greatest moral achievements man is capable of. But it is a *moral* achievement only if it is the result of an *individual's decision*, a decision not motivated by vanity, depression, or masochism, but by devotion to another person's life or to an idea. Few people have the courage and conviction to make this supreme sacrifice for the sake of an idea. The majority are not even willing to risk a job for the sake of their convictions. But if this decision is made not individually but nationally, it loses its ethical significance. It is not an authentic decision made by one person, but a decision made *for* millions by a few leaders who, in order to get the individuals to accept the "ethical" decisions, have to make them drunk with passions of hate and fear.

And for still another reason there is no truth to the "ethical" argument for war. I, as an individual, have a right to make the decision to end *my* life; I have no right to decide on the lives of others, of children, of unborn generations, of nations and of the human race itself. The death of one person is an individual event of no historical or social consequence. The destruction of part of the human race, and of its civilization, is immoral under any conditions. It makes a travesty of the greatest human capability, that of martyrdom, which is by its nature an act of individual decision, to use it as an appeal for the most immoral purpose—mass slaughter.

Not only is Kahn's position psychologically and morally naïve to say the least, but also politically. Not only is his whole discussion of atomic strategy conducted completely outside the political context of Russian–American relations and possibilities for a settlement, but in addition Kahn expresses his belief *"that a war is likely* [to] *continue a few days after the first strike and then to terminate* (*probably by negotiation*)"[31] and further that it "is part and parcel of *fighting* and *alleviating* a war that we must preserve enough offensive force either to destroy the enemy's offensive forces or to force him to negotiate."[32] To negotiate what? What are the peace aims? Why would not all the arguments which speak for continuation of the arms race be valid after the war is over? Why should one assume that three days after a mass slaughter negotiations are possible, when they seem to be impossible before any bomb has been dropped?

Clearly, from any sane point of view the possibilities of a humanly meaningful survival after a nuclear war are remote. Yet a dependence on deterrence for safeguarding peace rests, at the very best, on guesses and nothing more.

Against the view expressed here, that a nuclear war would be catastrophic, an objection has been raised

[31] H. Kahn, l.c. p. 107.
[32] H. Kahn, l.c. p. 108.

which we must take in account, especially since it comes from as influential a man as Henry A. Kissinger. The conviction that the continuation of the arms race will inevitably doom humanity "is bound," Kissinger writes, "to produce pressures for unilateral disarmament and therefore remove any incentive for serious negotiations on the part of the Communists."[33] First, facts are facts; if one is convinced—as a great number of experts are—that nuclear war would doom us, how can one *not* have an attitude of despair if negotiations to end the arms race fail? It is one thing to prove that the assumption of the fatal character of nuclear war is wrong, as Kahn attempts to do; but if one can not disprove Kahn's thesis, one can not recommend a hopeful attitude.

But even within his own frame of reference Kissinger is not right. The main consequence of insight into the catastrophic character of nuclear war is the demand for universal controlled disarmament, and *not* for unilateral disarmament. While it is arguable whether unilateral disarmament would give a tactical advantage to the Russians (although, according to those who propose it, this tactical advantage would be outweighed by important considerations), the main argument in this book, and of most American proponents of disarmament is for multilateral disarmament. By not mentioning multilateral disarmament, Kissinger presents a somewhat distorted picture, since the strongest argument for multilateral disarmament is precisely the catastrophic character of nuclear war. Insight into this fact is as important for the Russians as it is for the West, assuming the Russians are as rational as we are. In fact they have, in contrast to the Chinese, empha-

[33] Henry A. Kissinger, l.c. p. 285.

sized repeatedly that the danger of a "thermonuclear catastrophe" for the whole world is the main motive for universal disarmament. "Let us not approach the matter commercially," said Khrushchev, "and figure out the losses this or the other side would sustain. *War would be a calamity for all the peoples of the world.*

"Imagine what will happen when bombs begin to explode over cities. These bombs will not distinguish between Communists and non-Communists. . . . No, everything alive can be wiped out in the conflagration of nuclear explosions.

"Only an unreasonable person can be fearless of war in our day."

The idea of universal, unilateral disarmament is often confused with that of *arms control.* "Arms control" is considered by many to be the first step to disarmament, and if this were the essential function of arms control, there would be no serious objection to it. But the fact is that most of the arms control theorists do not look at it as a *real step to universal disarmament* but as a *substitute* for disarmament.[34]

Actually, arms control can be viewed as being related to the strategy of the invulnerable deterrent. Once both sides are invulnerable, it is in the interests of both to limit stockpiles and to keep other countries from obtaining atomic weapons. Yet for the military thinkers, proposals for even such modest arms control are made not without qualms. As Kissinger puts it: "Moreover, a feeling of despair should arms control prove unattainable would also be factually wrong. Without arms control stability will be more difficult to

[34] Cf. the excellent chapter on arms control by James P. Warburg, in *Disarmament: The Challenge of the Nineteen Sixties*, Doubleday, New York, 1961.

achieve. But it can probably be achieved even then. In the equation of retaliatory forces, advances in mobility will probably promote a degree of invulnerability even without a negotiated agreement."[35] It is clear from this quote which well represents the thinking of most military experts, that arms control is part of a theory of armament, not disarmament. In terms of the dangers of war, arms control represents defeatism and the full acceptance of the risks of total war, even though most of the arms control theorists, like Morgenstern, recognize that there can be no victors, perhaps few survivors, if the deterrent fails. In terms of national policy and its effect on the American people, the arguments for arms control aim toward another result, that of lulling us into a feeling of false security. A feeling of despair should arms control fail, we are told, would be "factually wrong."

As we have seen, to work at all, arms control—like the invulnerable deterrent—demands that we and our opponents act with a super-rationality, as though we were in a game. As one of the leading arms control theorists, Thomas Schelling, puts it: "Threats and responses to threats, reprisals and counter-reprisals, limited war, arms races, brinkmanship, surprise attack, trusting and cheating can be viewed as either hot-headed or cool-headed activities. In suggesting that they can usefully be viewed, in the development of theory, as cool-headed activities, it is not asserted that they are in fact entirely cool-headed. Rather it is asserted that the assumption of rational behavior is a productive one in the generation of systematic theory. If the behavior were actually cool-headed, valid and relevant theory would probably be easier to create than

[35] Henry A. Kissinger, l.c. p. 285.

it actually is. If we view our results as a bench mark for further approximation to reality, not as a fully adequate theory, we should manage to protect ourselves from the worst results of biased theory."[36]

Schelling goes on later to describe how arms control and strategic actions can be analyzed from the model of games, even though he acknowledges there are differences between games and these situations. But even with this qualification, Schelling and the other strategists who think in terms of the game theory are not approximating reality, but relinquishing it. The whole game analogy is based on a fundamental error with regard to the nature of games and the nature of nuclear war. It is the very nature of a game that each player, while he likes to win, is willing to accept the possibility of losing with equanimity; the loss is, by the very nature of the game, easily bearable, and far from being a threat to the existence of the players. The very thrill of the game lies, in fact, in the possibility of losing without having to fear that the loss will be devastating. If I were to put my entire future on a throw of the dice, or the turn of a roulette wheel, I would not be playing a game—I would be a desperate man.

For this very reason, the game theory can be satisfied with calculations that require plausibilities, probabilities, reasonable guesses. In matters of life and death, whether it is medicine or peace, one can not rely on guesses, because the consequences are too serious. The premise here is the very contrary to that of the game theory, namely that loss (which means an all-destruc-

---

[36] Cf. Thomas C. Schelling, *The Strategy of Conflict*, Harvard University Press, Cambridge, 1960, p. 16. Both Kissinger and Kahn quote Schelling and refer the reader to his analyses based on game theory.

tive war) is unacceptable, hence, here the game theory is not applicable.

But even in the unlikely case that the continuation of the arms race, controlled or not, *could prevent a nuclear war* within the next twenty-five years, what is the likely future of the social character of man in a bilateral or multilateral armed world, where, no matter how complex the problems or how full the satisfactions of any particular society, the biggest and most pervasive reality in any man's life is the poised missile, the humming data processor connected to it, the waiting radiation counters and seismographs, the over-all technocratic perfection (overlying the nagging but impotent fear of its imperfection) of the mechanism of holocaust?

To live for any length of time under the constant threat of destruction creates certain psychological effects in most human beings—fright, hostility, callousness, a hardening of the heart, and a resulting indifference to all the values we cherish. Such conditions will transform us into barbarians—though barbarians equipped with the most complicated machines. If we are serious in claiming that our aim is to preserve freedom (that is, to prevent the subordination of the individual under an all-powerful state), we *must admit that this freedom will be lost, whether the deterrent works or does not work.*

A similar idea is expressed by Charles E. Osgood.[37] "I have come to the somber conclusion," Osgood writes, "that we would not be able to maintain a favorable position in this race without giving up our way of life as rapidly as possible. Then we could be able to chan-

[37] *A Case for Graduated Unilateral Disengagement,* Bulletin of the Atomic Scientists, April 1960, p. 127 ff.

nel the energies of our people into military preparation, order our young people into training in the physical sciences, and make decisions and changes in strategy without democratic processes."

George Kennan has expressed his ideas about the results of the continuation of the arms race in his Reith
Lectures delivered over the BBC in England. "But beyond this," Kennan states, "what sort of a life is it to
which these devotees of the weapons race would see
us condemned? The technological realities of this competition are constantly changing from month to month
and from year to year. Are we to flee like haunted
creatures from one defensive device to another, each
more costly and humiliating than the one before, cow-
ering underground one day, breaking up our cities the
next, attempting to surround ourselves with elaborate
electronic shields on the third, concerned only to pro-
long the length of our lives while sacrificing all the
values for which it might be worth while to live at all?
If I thought that this was the best the future held for
us, I should be tempted to join those who say 'Let us
divest ourselves of this weapon altogether; let us stake
our safety on God's grace and our own good con-
sciences and on that measure of common sense and
humanity which even our adversaries possess; but then
let us at least walk like men, with our heads up, so
long as we are permitted to walk at all.' We must not
forget that this is actually the situation in which many
of the peoples of this world are obliged to live today;
and while I would not wish to say that they are now
more secure than we are, for the fact that they do not
hold these weapons, I would submit that they are more
secure than we would be if we were to resign ourselves
entirely to the negative dynamics of the weapons race,
as many would have us do.

Suggestions for peace

"The beginning of understanding rests, in this appalling problem, with the recognition that the weapon of mass destruction is a sterile and hopeless weapon which may for a time serve as an answer of sorts to itself and as an uncertain sort of shield against utter cataclysm, but which can not in any way serve the purposes of a constructive and hopeful foreign policy. The true end of political action is, after all, to affect the deeper convictions of men; this the atomic bomb can not do. The suicidal nature of this weapon renders it unsuitable both as a sanction of diplomacy and as the basis of an alliance. Such a weapon is simply not one with which one can usefully support political desiderata; nor is it one with which one readily springs to the defense of one's friends. There can be no coherent relations between such weapons and the normal objects of national policy. A defense posture built around a weapon suicidal in its implications can serve in the long run only to paralyze national policy, to undermine alliances, and to drive everyone deeper and deeper into the hopeless exertions of the weapons race."[38]

To sum up: it is true that the aim of universal controlled disarmament is exceedingly difficult to reach; maybe it is unrealistic, as its opponents say. But to believe that a strategy of mutual threats with ever-more destructive weapons can, in the long run, prevent a nuclear war, and that a society following this road could preserve its democratic character, is a great deal more unrealistic. It is, indeed, one of the irrationalities of human nature that we are prone to seek for easier, short-term solutions because we are afraid of the difficulties of the fundamental and real solutions. But in

[38] George F. Kennan *Russia, The Atom and the West,* Harper & Bros., New York, 1957, 1958, pp. 54–55.

individual or in social life, it is the logic of facts that
determines reality, not the logic of wishful thinking.

II) AMERICAN–RUSSIAN ALLIANCE
AGAINST CHINA AND
THE COLONIAL PEOPLES

To those who have followed the argument about the
conservative nature of the Russian system and about
the threat to Russia as well as to the United States by
the Asian, African, and Latin American revolutions under the leadership of China, it will not sound too unreasonable to propose another way to peace that may
enjoy increasing favor in the near future. Why should
not the Soviet Union and the United States be able to
form a close military and political alliance, force the
Chinese government (by the threat of nuclear attack)
to accept disarmament, prevent the smaller states (also
if necessary by force) from acquiring thermonuclear
weapons, and organize the world under American–
Russian domination? (It would not matter whether this
American–Russian domination of the world were
called World Government, United Nations, or whatever.) This idea may be tempting to some military and
political leaders both in the Soviet Union and in the
United States, because it is an essentially conservative
idea, it leaves the power in the hands of the military
groups, and it does not require any basic change in the
American or the Russian systems. Yet, I believe this solution is most undesirable and, what is more important, practically impossible. It is undesirable because it
would mean the establishment of a most reactionary
world dictatorship exercised by the two greatest powers. Such a dictatorship would have to curb all revolutionary movements among the Asian, African, and

Latin American peoples, and hence it would have to build a dictatorial police system in order to stop a historical process, which in the long run can not be stopped by force. Such a system might save the world from immediate nuclear war, but since by its very nature it would require a fully armed United States and Soviet Union, it could hardly prevent the outbreak of war eventually, when Russian–American confidence will have worn thin.

There is, however, hardly any need to consider the advantages and disadvantages of such a new "holy alliance," because it is clearly unacceptable to the Soviet Union. Not primarily because it would be too difficult for the Soviet Union to change its ideological position so drastically that there would be no visible break. This could be done by accusing China of having betrayed communism, etc., and "proving" why the "peace-loving" circles in the United States are to be preferred to the "adventurist" elements in China who want to start a world war with the aim of world domination by China; to take this line would be difficult, but not impossible. But the reason why a United States–Soviet Union "holy alliance" seems impossible lies not in the field of ideas, but in that of political facts. While the Soviet Union today feels menaced by an ever-growing China, her position vis-à-vis the West is nevertheless greatly strengthened by the existence of China and by the strength of the colonial peoples. If the Soviet Union were to give up her role as an ally of China and as the spokesman for the aspirations of the colonial peoples, she would face the combined American–Western European alliance alone and without support, and would have to fear that her "allies" would attack the Soviet Union after China and the colonial peoples had been disarmed. For these reasons it seems quite clear that such an alliance is unacceptable to the Russians, and hence is not a feasible possibility for peace. The ending of the cold war can bring about a greater independence of the Soviet Union from her Chinese ally, but all attempts to split the two powers and to break the alliance will be repelled by the Russians for reasons of sheer survival.

III) A PROPOSAL FOR PEACE

a) Universal controlled disarmament

If it is true that the policy of the arms race (controlled or not) will most likely result in thermonuclear war, and that, even if the "stable deterrent" could prevent such a war, the arms race will result in militarized, frightened, dictatorial societies, then the first condition for the possibility of peace and democracy is *universal controlled disarmament*. This would hold true even if the United States, Britain, France, and the Soviet Union were the only owners of nuclear weapons. However, nobody doubts that a great number of other countries—China, Germany, India, Israel, Sweden, etc.—will have the capability to produce thermonuclear weapons in the near future, and that this spread of nuclear weapons will still further reduce the possibilities for peace.

In discussing this danger of the "nth country" having nuclear weapons, it seems worth while to make a point that is often overlooked. Small countries like Israel or Sweden could, of course, explode their thermonuclear bombs either by accident or because of the irrationality of their leaders, but they can hardly make their nuclear power part of their *policy*. The much greater danger lies in the extension of nuclear armament to other great powers, especially China, Germany, and Japan, since those countries, like the present members of the "atomic club," would use their military power as an adjunct to their political ambitions. Thus the chance of nuclear war as a result of mutual threats in the context of such over-all political strategy would be considerably enhanced.

How then can these powers be prevented from acquiring nuclear weapons? It is true that, thus far, the Soviet Union has not given these weapons to China, and Germany has no nuclear weapons. But considering the course we are taking in Germany, it is likely that the Germans will soon have nuclear weapons as members of NATO, and even independently. If this happens, the Russians will not be able or willing to restrain China from becoming a nuclear power, which, in turn, will lead to the nuclear armament of Japan.

It is, of course, possible that the United States and the Soviet Union could prevent these countries by economic or even military pressure from acquiring nuclear arms. But this would mean a Russo–American alliance, directed against China (and Germany), which is most unlikely for reasons which were discussed above. It seems that the only way to prevent the spread of nuclear weapons to the other great countries is by global disarmament, in which all the great countries would participate.

This seems to be the idea behind Khrushchev's disarmament proposal; he seems to see the alternative clearly: either universal disarmament or acceleration of the arms race between the United States and the Soviet Union, plus nuclear armament of countries such as Germany, China, Japan. It is unfortunate that so far the Western reaction to the disarmament proposals has been lukewarm. The West has not declined universal disarmament outright, but it has also never fully accepted it as a practical goal. The Russians, in their turn, are not willing to accept inspection by which they would lose one of their military advantages, namely the factor of secrecy, in exchange for a limited "arms control" which would only be another form of prolonging the arms race. (At the last "Pugwash" Conference held in Moscow, the American scientists suggested a compromise, namely that inspection would increase in the same proportion as disarmament increases, and the Russians were receptive to this idea as a basis for discussion.)

It is important under these circumstances to ask oneself why the West so far has not been willing to consider universal disarmament seriously. One stock answer which is usually given is that the Russians do not permit inspection. But this answer is not tenable in view of the fact that they have repeatedly declared that they are willing to permit any kind of inspection provided the West accepts universal disarmament as the concrete and immediate goal; at least we must negotiate in order to find out if they are serious about inspection. However, I am not recommending a method of suspicious and perfunctory negotiations in which each step is conditional upon ironclad guarantees. I believe that unilateral initiatives toward disarmament are necessary to generate an atmosphere in which genuine negotiations become possible. (Some such unilateral steps have been outlined in detail by Charles Osgood in *The Bulletin of Atomic Scientists,* Vol. 16, No. 4, and by myself in *Daedalus,* Vol. 89, No. 4.) Furthermore, we must be aware of the fact that there is no foolproof system of inspection, but that the risks of an inspections system are smaller than those of the armament race. In considering the pros and cons of inspection systems, we must also give some weight to their contribution to an atmosphere of legality. In leading the Russians and ourselves into the formal observance of agreed-upon rules—even if it is only a symbolic observance—we make it harder for either side to break the rules thereafter and flout the hopes for peace and legality that have been generated on both sides. Is it that we see less clearly than the Russians the dangers of an atomically armed world, or is it that we are so caught in our picture of their "wish for world domination" that we can not believe that they mean what they say? Or is it that we are afraid that we could not cope with the economic consequences disarmament would have for our system? Or is it that the armed services, being opposed to disarmament, have already such power that they can prevent even a serious consideration of disarmament?[39]

Since this is a matter of life or death for the United States and the rest of the world, it would seem to be of the utmost importance to examine not only, as we usually do, the possible flaws in the Russian posture, but also the possible reasons for our refusal to consider disarmament more seriously.

b) American–Russian modus vivendi on the basis of the status quo

Even if it is admitted that universal disarmament is a necessary condition for the preservation of peace and freedom, how is disarmament possible, unless the cold war is ended first? How can either of the two powers seriously negotiate disarmament as long as each suspects the other of wanting to destroy it? The answer is clear; *no political understanding is possible or prac-*

[39] Cf. the statement by Harrison Brown and James Real, *Community of Fear*, Center for the Study of Democratic Institutions, Santa Barbara, 1960, p. 28.

*tical so long as the mutual threat of extinction exists,
and at the same time disarmament is not possible unless a political understanding is reached.* It is a moot
question to ask what comes first; both problems must
be tackled together, and it may even be expected that
in searching for a way to solve the political problem
it will be easier to find a way to solve the disarmament
problem—and vice versa.

Walter Millis has put the same question in a very
succinct way. "The Soviet Union," he writes, "is very
much interested in disarmament. It probably wants
disarmament to relieve its internal economic problems;
it is probably as anxious as anyone in the West to escape the nuclear threat; but it is certainly interested
in the political uses that can be made of 'disarmament'
in the current international context. The true Western
answer, it seems to me, to the Soviet position on disarmament is not to allege bad faith, *but to ask how
the Soviet Union conceives that the power struggle will
be conducted under the provisions it proposes.* And I
believe that the Soviet Union is entitled to serve the
same demand upon the West. Neither of the two great
power centers is prepared today to provide an answer
to such a demand. Both, on the other hand, are clearly
groping toward one. If it is discovered, the world problem will be solved. If it is not, most of us will probably
die of blast and radiation disease, and our survivors
will live a very poor life on a globe somewhat less suit-
able than the present one for human habitation."[40]

I shall now attempt to answer Millis's question:
namely, how the power struggle between the United

[40] Walter Millis, *Permanent Peace,* Center for the Study
of Democratic Institutions, Santa Barbara, 1961, p. 31.
(My italics, E.F.)

States and the Soviet Union can be conducted under conditions of disarmament.

The first condition for a political understanding is to overcome the hysterical and irrational misconceptions the two blocs have about each other. As I have tried to show, the Soviet Union is a conservative, totalitarian, managerialism, and not a revolutionary system with the aim of world domination; Khrushchev is not the successor of Marx or of Lenin, as for reasons of his own political position he has to claim. *We* no longer have a capitalistic system of individual initiative, free competition, minimal government intervention. We are now also a bureaucratic industrial society.

It seems, indeed, as if the only point on which East and West agree are the clichés about each other. To disagree with this agreement is the beginning of a realistic understanding. The next step lies in the knowledge that there are no important economic or even political conflicts between the two power blocs which in themselves would constitute a reason for war; that the only danger that might bring about a war is mutual fear resulting from the arms race, and from ideological differences.

What, then, is the realistic basis for an American–Russian understanding? Actually, the answer is eminently simple. *The basis is the mutual recognition of the status quo, the mutual agreement not to change the existing political balance of power between the two blocs.*

This means first of all that the West must give up any design to change the present Russian possessions and spheres of interest in Eastern Europe, and that the Soviet Union does the same with regard to the West. It is perfectly true that Russia gained control over her satellites by force, and as a result of a victorious war.

It is true that it might have been possible by means of greater insistence at the end of the last war to save some of these countries from Russian domination; but all these are futile considerations now.

It is obvious that the Soviet Union will not relinquish what she has without a war. No great power at the height of its strength—whether Communist or capitalist —has ever done this.[41] No Russian political leader who arranged such a deal could survive politically; the idea of "being liberated" in a war in which their countries would be devastated is clearly not something the satellite nations would want, and it is certainly also not our own intention. Yet, in view of the fact that the satellite nations, as the various rebellions have shown, are among the weakest points in the Russian structure, the Soviet leaders are most sensitive to any direct or indirect menace from them. Hence our position of not recognizing the present Russian possessions is one of the factors preventing an understanding. At the same time, our position not only does not lead to greater freedom for one single person in the satellite countries. If anything, it prevents the process of liberalization. Events have shown that while the leaders of the Soviet Union will never permit any one of the satellite states to leave the Russian orbit, as far as foreign policy is concerned, they are willing to permit them a certain amount of independence in internal affairs, especially with a lessening of tension between the two blocs.

[41] The example of Great Britain giving up India is no exception: It was a declining empire which gave up India under the leadership of a less imperialistically minded and hence more objective Labour Government. On the other hand, compare the attitude of the British in the Suez adventure, the attitude of the Dutch in Indonesia, the French in Algeria, and the Belgians in the Congo.

Suggestions for peace

It is in this context that the question of Berlin must be understood. There is no evidence that the Russians want to incorporate West Berlin into the Eastern Zone; however, they are vitally interested in securing the stability of their sphere of interest in East Germany. Khrushchev's diplomatic gambit is to threaten the West with regard to Berlin where *he* has the advantage, in order to force the West to accept his position in East Germany where the West can cause him a lot of trouble. The solution of the Berlin problem lies in the full recognition of Russia's satellites, including East Germany, in exchange for the full guarantee for the independent existence of Berlin as part of the Western world.

What stands in the way of the acceptance of the Russian possessions in Eastern Europe? Here we come across some of the paradoxes and irrationalities of political thinking. On the one hand, it is evident to and admitted by every responsible writer, that the West has no intention of liberating any of the satellites by force; more than that, it is equally evident that the West does not even desire any anti-Communist revolution in East Germany, since that would force the West to either send assistance—and that means risking general war—or to accept the humiliating position of failing to help the revolution. Why, then, does the Western alliance not accept the status quo formally and unequivocally? Or, on the other hand, why are the Russians not satisfied with American *de facto* acceptance of a status quo? Why do they insist on more formal and binding agreements, like a peace treaty?

The answer to both sets of questions lies in the same fact, the existence of a dynamic and expansionist Germany. The Russians believe that it is West Germany that threatens their Western sphere of interest, and that the United States policy is a threat mainly insofar as it follows the German line. I have tried to show in a previous chapter that this fear of future German aggression is by no means unfounded. Even though it is not a danger today, it will be one tomorrow.

It is a fact that the majority of the inhabitants of East Germany are living under a regime they do not want, and that this regime is obnoxious to all who love political freedom. Hence, the decision to reconcile oneself to the continuation of Communist rule in East Germany is a hard one for those who truly cherish freedom. (It should not be so hard for those who reconcile themselves quite easily to anti-Russian dictatorships.) But, if one faces the dilemma realistically, then there remains only one answer: to accept the facts as they are in the knowledge that the aim of avoiding war is from every standpoint more important than that of a "liberated" East Germany. The irony of it is that there is no such alternative, since the real choice is only between a Communist-dominated or a destroyed East Germany.

The ideological argument centers on such questions as the national feeling of the Germans in favor of unification. Is it not time that we should begin to question the shibboleth of "German national unity"? German unity began only ninety years ago, as a result of Bismarck's statesmanship. Even Bismarck intentionally left out Austria and preferred a solution which did not unite all Germans. On the other hand, it was Hitler whose aggressive aims were based on the demand for the unification of all Germans. If it is necessary to unite East Germany with West Germany, why not also Austria, Tyrol, the Sudetenland, Alsace, Silesia, East Prussia? Are we not following the same course that was followed by England and France between 1933 and

1938 when they accepted Hitler's demand for the incorporation of all German-speaking peoples in one country, and when they did not recognize that these national demands were only the ideological preparations for a war of conquest?

The West German government knows quite well that Germany can not be reunited, short of a war. But it keeps the demand alive as a means of sustaining nationalist feelings and of preventing a political understanding between the United States and the Soviet Union. Because we are obsessed by the idea of the Russian menace and thus of the need for German aid, we are driven to support a German policy that in the long run makes a political settlement with Russia impossible—and hence makes peace improbable.

We must attempt to free ourselves from purely ideological clichés. If "a separate state there [East Germany]—even were it non-Communist—runs against the German national 'feeling',"[42] why do we have to adjust to this "national feeling" which is largely synthetic anyway? Why is it that "we cannot surrender the right of the German people to determine its own fate at a time not too far distant?"[43] Is this not another way of saying that we must permit German expansionism to have its own way? Why is it that solutions which safeguard the status of Berlin "in return for the recognition of East Germany, would be an enormous communist victory?"[44]

Because of our obsession with the Russian wish for world domination (and maybe also because of many

[42] Henry A. Kissinger, *The Necessity for Choice*, Harper & Bros., New York, 1960, p. 131.

[43] l.c. p. 137.

[44] l.c. p. 144.

American–German financial interests) we tend to accept the demands of West Germany and thus we make an over-all settlement with Russia impossible. There is much talk that making concessions to the Soviet Union is a repetition of the appeasement policy toward Hitler. I believe that, if one insists on drawing a present-day analogy to the appeasement policy toward Nazi Germany, it lies in *our present appeasement of Adenauer's Germany.*

Basically, French and British policy toward Hitler from 1933 to 1938 was not unrelated to the idea that Hitler's expansion could be deflected from the West to the East. Those who were against appeasement, like Churchill, recognized that Hitler would not be satisfied only with expansion toward the East. Today, when our whole foreign policy is based on the idea that we must defend ourselves militarily against the Russian menace, we again appease Germany. We give in to her ever-increasing demands for armament, and allow Adenauer to influence our policy in such a way that a peaceful understanding with the Soviet Union becomes very difficult. There are even some reasons to believe that soon Germany will become so strong that many American political and military leaders will think it is too late to stop her, even if we wish to. Are we really so naïve as to see only the Germany of today, and not to visualize the Germany of tomorrow, which we are helping to bring to life?

As far as recognition of the mutual status quo in Europe is concerned, my proposition is to accept unequivocally the present status quo, and to curb any further German rearmament.

In this connection let us turn to our Berlin policy. The cliché is to say how uncompromising and aggressive Khrushchev's position over Berlin is. What are the facts? Khrushchev demanded that West Berlin should be made a free city; he intimated his willingness to accept United Nations control or even a four-power control over the free city. He never demanded that West Berlin should be incorporated into East Germany. As I have said before, his demand was essentially meant to force the West into a recognition of East Germany, and the discontinuation of further German rearmament. Aware that even these two aims were not attainable, he seemed willing to be satisfied, at least for a transitory period, with some small concessions on the part of the West.

These concessions, mostly suggested by the West at the Four Ministers' Conference in 1959, were: a reduction of the number of soldiers in Berlin (since these soldiers have more symbolic than military value, it really matters little whether there are 12,000 or 7000); agreement not to store atomic weapons in Berlin (they have never been stored there); and agreement to stop conducting subversive propaganda against Russia from West Berlin.

While these concessions were never formalized, they were obviously the basis for the "Camp David atmosphere" during Khrushchev's visit in Washington, and for President Eisenhower's remark at the time that the Berlin situation was "abnormal." Khrushchev returned to Moscow, praised Eisenhower and the success of his visit. What happened then? Perhaps under the influence of pressure from Adenauer, perhaps under the impression that Russia would not risk war over Berlin, we announced (in Mr. Dillon's speech) that all concessions were off, and that we were not any longer willing to compromise as had been indicated during Khrushchev's visit in Washington.

Khrushchev's reaction was an aggressive speech in

Baku. We then inflicted another defeat on Khrushchev, although probably more through maladroitness than by design, by our reaction to the U-2 incident. While Khrushchev tried at first to save the situation by declaring that he believed President Eisenhower did not know anything about it, the President countered by taking full responsibility for the flight, and declaring that it had been justified. What was Khrushchev supposed to do? Can we be surprised that he felt personally slapped-down and, more importantly, that he had to react to this defeat in a way that preserved his position in Russia? Khrushchev left the summit meeting in a huff, made aggressive speeches, and later insulted the President. But on the central issue, that of Berlin, he indicated in his speech in that city a few days later that he would keep his original promise not to force the issue. He made no threats, and postponed the whole issue for discussion with the new United States administration. Khrushchev's behavior in this whole affair was essentially defensive, unless one is naïve enough to assume that shouting is politically more significant than action.[45]

If an American–Russian modus vivendi on the basis of the status quo in Europe sounds difficult, such an understanding with regard to the rest of the world will easily appear next to impossible. Yet there is no denying the fact that unless it can be achieved there will be continued tension and a continued armament race —and the probability of a thermonuclear war.

[45] Walter Lippmann in his interview with Khrushchev (April 1961) made it very clear in Mr. Khrushchev's mind that the future of Germany is the key question. "And for two reasons: 1) because of the danger of Germany's atomic armament, 2) because of the need for a peace treaty defining the frontiers of Poland and Czechoslovakia and stabilizing the existence of the East German State."

That such an understanding should be possible requires, of course, in the first place, that neither side has the intention of conquering the world. I do not have to prove to the American reader that world conquest is not the intention of the United States. That it is not the intention of the Soviet Union either, I have tried to show in a previous chapter. But how can the two blocs arrive at an agreement on the maintenance of the status quo in Asia, Africa, and Latin America when these parts of the world are in a continuous ferment, both politically and socio-economically? Would such an agreement, even if it could be arrived at, not mean freezing the present power structure all over the world, stabilizing what can not remain stable? Does it not mean an international guarantee for the continued existence of some of the most reactionary regimes which are bound to fall sooner or later?

This difficulty will appear less formidable if one considers that an agreement not to alter the present possessions and spheres of interest between the United States and the Soviet Union and China, is not the same as freezing the *internal* structure of all Asiatic, African, and Latin American states. It means, in fact, that nations, even though they change their government and their social structure, do not, for this reason, change their allegiance from one bloc to the other.

There are a number of examples showing that this is possible; the most striking one is Egypt. Egypt, which was one of the poorest countries in the world and, in addition, one of the most corruptly governed was bound to have a revolution.

Like all other revolutions in Asia and Africa, the Egyptian had two aspects: it was intensely nationalistic, and it was socialistic in a broad sense, aiming at basic economic changes for the benefit of the broad masses of the Egyptian population. Nasser had to free himself from the remnants of British domination, but he was resolved not to fall under Russian domination either. He took the only reasonable course, that of non-alignment, exploiting the rivalry between the two blocs to his advantage and for the political survival of an independent Egypt.

It is hardly exaggerated to say that United States foreign policy as it was then formulated by the late Mr. Dulles almost drove Nasser into the Russian camp. Neutrality, according to this doctrine, was immoral, and friendly relations on the part of a small power like Egypt toward the Soviet Union were considered to be hostile to the United States and were to be punished accordingly.[46] (In the case of Egypt the abrupt withdrawal of the promised loan for the Assuan Dam.) Yet Nasser remained neutral, even in spite of the extreme Anglo-French military provocation of the Suez attack.

The same holds true for Iraq, Lebanon, Indonesia. In Iraq and in Lebanon, the United States seemed convinced that a new government would slip into the Soviet orbit, and we prepared for military intervention, but the State Department's prognosis failed to materialize. The United States attitude was then justified as having "prevented" the Soviets from taking over these countries, even though it is very unlikely that there had been such intentions, and even less so that the respective countries want to be taken over by the Soviets.

The United States position of trying to enforce the continuance of "pro-Western governments" in countries where these governments are definitely unpopular

[46] The last outstanding example of the Dulles policy was Mr. Herter's treatment of Ghana's president during his visit to New York in 1960, which is in marked contrast to Mr. Kennedy's treatment of Ghana's president a year later.

is, in the long run, doomed to failure. The only constructive policy lies in permitting and even furthering the emergence of a bloc of nonaligned, neutral countries. Only in this way can acute American–Russian conflicts with accompanying threats of using nuclear force be avoided.

The Russians have actually acted more wisely in this respect than we: they accept neutrality as a sufficient condition for friendly relations and economic help. It is time for the United States to adopt the same attitude. It is one of the most promising features of the Kennedy administration that it shows a definite turn in this direction, at least as far as Asia and Africa are concerned. The point of my argument is to emphasize how vitally important this change is, and that it must not be made halfheartedly.

Discussing the need for accepting and furthering the political neutrality of large parts of the underdeveloped world is, however, only the beginning. The political stance of these countries can not be separated from their internal social and economic development. It is precisely here where a more realistic attitude is necessary.

The Western powers, like the Communists, talk in terms of the choice between capitalism and communism. This alternative is almost the one thing the two camps agree on. The facts are, however, more complex. Capitalism in the middle of the twentieth century is not the capitalism of individual initiative, minimal state activity, etc., that it was in the nineteenth century. Both the Russian and the Chinese types of communism—different as they are from each other—are quite different from the Marxist socialism they each pretend to resemble. What are the facts and the realistic possibilities?

First, we must recognize that the underdeveloped countries, in the long run, will not choose capitalism for both economic and psychological reasons. They can not choose a system that was developed in Europe over several hundreds of years, in response to the particular historical conditions of that continent. These underdeveloped countries need a system which fulfills these conditions: first, economic power must be taken from the small cliques who use it only for their own interests and without regard for the needs of the majority of the population; second, the economy must follow a plan that allocates resources in the interests of, and for the optimal development of the entire economy.

The cardinal point is that the alternative in the underdeveloped countries is precisely *not* that between capitalism and communism, an alternative which the Russians and the Chinese are fond of proposing, but that the alternative is *which kind of socialism will they choose:* the Russian state managerialism, the Chinese anti-individualistic communism, or a humanistic, democratic socialism, which attempts to combine the necessary minimum of bureaucratic centralization with the optimum of individual initiative, participation and responsibility.

If the West insists on the communist-capitalist alternative, if it allies itself with outmoded reactionary regimes which are doomed by history, then it will help the Russians—or more likely the Chinese—to gain the leadership of two-thirds—and within a generation, almost four-fifths of the human race. The poor peoples of the world will believe that they must choose the way which is allowing China to develop at twice the rate of India, provided there is no other alternative.

But in spite of all Chinese propaganda, there is plenty of evidence that the Chinese way of complete and ruthless regimentation is not what most of these peoples prefer. The wish for freedom and independence is not—as it is sometimes alleged—a relatively recent Western discovery; it is a deep-rooted need in the very existence of man, but it is not the only one. If it has to compete with hunger, fear, and hopelessness, most people—in the East and in the West—will be willing to sell out their desire for freedom. The question is whether such a choice can be avoided.

Furthermore, even if millions of peasants in all these countries have lived, thus far, under such abysmal conditions of hunger and hopelessness that at the moment they cannot be fully interested in freedom, this has less political significance than many people believe. The history of the underdeveloped countries is being made by relatively small groups of an educated, middle-class élite, who do appreciate the dangers and the evils of totalitarianism. It is in fact quite remarkable how well India and other parts of Asia as well as of Latin America and Africa have stood up against the seduction of communism. But it is also clear that the younger generation will become increasingly impatient if the necessary fundamental reforms are not made.

My proposal that the only solution for the underdeveloped countries is democratic-socialist systems, adapted to the needs of each country, and varying accordingly just as Yugoslavia varies from India, is by no means a theoretical construction. The fact is that, as Barnett puts it, "Marxism has had a deep and widespread influence among intellectuals in many countries in the area [South and Southeast Asia]. Most of the leaders in South and Southeast Asia subscribe to 'socialism' of one kind or another. Many hope to create societies which can best be described as 'socialist de-

mocracies,' combining free and representative government with varying degrees of state economic planning.
For the most part, they still look primarily to the West
for their models, and they are attempting to adapt
Western experience to their own needs, but few accept
any specific Western model without qualification, and
they have encountered great difficulties in attempting
to transplant Western institutions in their countries.
Many, while rejecting communism as a system of
power, have felt that the Communists' experience in
the Soviet Union and China has considerable relevance
to their own problems."[47]

The problem is whether these leaders can eventually find a democratic-socialist pattern which will
show achievements comparable to those of China, or
whether they will have to accept the Communist solution which they would prefer to avoid. Their decision
depends at least as much on the attitude of the West
as it does on Communist propaganda.

So far, the West has been the most effective propa-
gandist for the Communists, by insisting that the Communists are the true heirs of Marx, and that there is
no alternative other than capitalism. The United States
has made this error more than Europe, because Europe is at least familiar with democratic socialist ideas
and parties, which up to 1960 have ruled at one time
or another, since 1918, in Great Britain, France, Germany, Belgium, Italy, the Netherlands, Denmark, Nor-
way, Sweden, and Iceland.

In many of these countries the socialists were defeated in recent years because the conservative parties
adopted part of the socialist program, and because the
socialists themselves stagnated in the midst of plenty.

[47] A. Doak Barnett, l.c. p. 298.

But it would be a serious mistake to believe that socialism in the underdeveloped countries is finished because it is at the moment on the defensive in the rich countries. In fact it may be considered one of the most important tasks of democratic socialists in Europe to help democratic socialism in the underdeveloped countries and to interpret it to the West.

There is an objection to the idea suggested here which is serious enough to warrant immediate attention. This objection runs along the following lines: if it is the aim of the underdeveloped countries to achieve economic well-being within a few generations, if they want to build an industry of their own and provide the majority of their inhabitants with a standard of living that can at least be compared with the poorer European countries, how can they do it except in the Chinese way: totalitarian organization, force, and mass-suggestion?

Are their leaders not forced to create a spirit of fanaticism and fear in order to sustain voluntary underconsumption? I believe this is not necessarily so. There is, of course, the problem of mobilizing the human energy to achieve a far higher economic productivity than these countries have now. The West officially claims that the hope of monetary gain is the most important way, and no doubt, this motive is effective within a certain frame of reference. (The Russians also agree—in practice.) But there are other ways of mobilizing human energy. There is the Chinese way of total mobilization of brain, heart, and brawn by force and suggestion; and this way seems to work, although at the expense of fundamental human values. There is still another way, which democratic, humanist socialism offers: an appeal to the sense of self-respect, individual initiative, social responsibility, and pride of the individual.

If such an appeal were merely ideological and fictitious it would have no real and lasting effect. But if it is based on the real possibilities the system offers for these qualities to develop; if, furthermore, such an appeal is made in a system that has a plan and in which individual effort contributes to the progress of the society as a whole, then, I believe, that human energy can be mobilized to an extent comparable to totalitarian systems.[48]

What matters is, as I have stressed before, not only the psychic needs and desires of the broad masses but also the character structure of the educated middle-class élite. What is their motivation? Is it necessarily that of material wealth, the Western businessman's motivation in the nineteenth and twentieth centuries? If this is so, the only possible outcome can be that of corrupt government bureaucracies. For if it is wealth the leaders of underdeveloped countries are after, they will have to enrich themselves at the expense of the masses—possible only through deceit and oppression.

But there are many examples that wealth is by no means the only motivating force for the new élites, and, in fact, for some old ones. The governing groups in Yugoslavia and Egypt, the very top leadership in India, and the Chinese leadership, according to all reports, are not corrupt. (By this, I do not mean that they do not have a higher standard of living than the majority,

[48] Yugoslavia, which has a rate of annual industrial growth (9 per cent) similar to that of the Soviet Union, is an impressive example; while Yugoslavia does not have a two-party system or elections in the Western sense, it has no political terror and its system furthers individual activity and responsibility and encourages decentralization.

but that their privileges are definitely limited, and not arrived at through theft and bribery.) What is apparently a strong motivation among these new leaders is a pride in their skill in administration and organization. In contrast to the traditional monetary motivation of the entrepreneur, the new élites are motivated by the same factors that motivate many professional men and women in our system: the satisfaction of applying an acquired skill and of obtaining useful results.

We in the West often forget that satisfaction in workmanship, in the successful application of one's skills, can be at least as strong an incentive as profit.

In addition to the individual satisfaction rooted in skillful performance, the new élites need and often have another potent satisfaction—that of a sense of social obligation and solidarity with the broad masses of their respective countries. This usually takes the form of national pride; whether we think of China, or of Egypt, or of any one of the newly awakened countries, they are led by men with a genuine national feeling, often bordering on an irrational nationalism. Professional and national pride, together with a sense of social justice and responsibility, may be said to be the most important motivations of the new leaders of many of the underdeveloped countries. From a psychological standpoint, these motivations are just as potent and as real as the desire for money and the lust for power; they are just as much a part of human nature as the latter ones. What matters is which kind of motivation a given society encourages and furthers, or, to put it differently, what kind of personality will rise to the top.

The question arises whether the new élite is more prone to accept the Russian, the Chinese, or a democratic form of socialism. This is difficult to answer. But one thing seems certain: which course the new élite will take depends on two factors, one psychological and one economic. These new leaders are proud and sensitive; they resent the treatment they have been given by the Western powers for more than a century. (The Russian leaders showed the same kind of sensitivity, especially before they had achieved their present success.) They have not forgotten the humiliation of the opium war, the slave trade, and also the American "banana policy." They react in a perfectly normal way, being sensitive and even sometimes supersensitive and thus prone to take an aggressive anti-Western posture when the West continues to treat them with overt or slightly hidden arrogance. The tone of moral superiority toward the underdeveloped countries, which permeates many of our statements, serves only to create a deep antagonism toward the West, and to increase their tendency to unite with the Communist bloc.

There is more than that. The West presents a picture of moral bankruptcy to the "new world." We preached Christianity to the "heathen" while we were taking them for slaves and treating them as inferiors; now we preach spirituality, morality, faith in God, and freedom, while our effective values (and it is part of our system of "doublethink" that we also preach them) are money and consumption. Unless we experience an authentic renaissance of our professed values, we shall only create antagonism in those whom we have held in contempt. Only a drastic change in our attitude toward the Asian, African, and Latin American countries can do away with their deep suspicion of our motives and of our sincerity.

In addition to this psychological factor is the economic one. If the new countries must achieve industrialization without considerable foreign aid, they may choose the Chinese way of complete control over and utilization of their "human capital." But, if they were to receive economic aid from the West, they are likely to prefer a more humane and democratic way. Some of the new leaders may be bought; but they will be exceptions. The majority will go ahead, attempting to further the development of their peoples. Their attitude toward the West will depend mostly on ourselves, on our capacity to break entirely with our colonialist past, psychologically, and on the economic and technical aid we are willing to give them freely without trying to force them into a political alliance with us.

Will these countries then become democratic, "free" countries? It is most unfortunate that, as I noted before, the words "democracy" and "freedom" are used so much in a ritualistic sense and with a great deal of insincerity. Many of our "freedom-loving" allies are dictatorships, and we seem to care little whether a country is a democracy or not, as long as it is a political and military ally against the Communist bloc. But aside from this opportunistic insincerity, we also take a shallow and superficial view of democracy. The political concept of democracy and freedom has developed during several hundreds of years of European history. It is the result of the victory against monarchical autocracy, achieved by the great revolutions in England and France. The essence of this concept is that no irresponsible monarch has the right to decide the fate of the people, but only the people themselves; its aim is "government of the people, by the people, for the people."

But democracy was not born in one day. Throughout most of the nineteenth century, as in England for example, the right to vote was restricted to those who owned property; while in the United States even today there are a considerable number of Negroes who are practically disenfranchised. Yet on the whole, with the economic and social development of the last hundred years, universal suffrage has been generally accepted in most of the Western countries.

A system that permits free and unrestricted political activities and truly free elections is the most desirable one, even if it has its shortcomings. But this is only one aspect of democracy. It can not easily be transferred to different social systems, which have no middle class, a small degree of literacy, or are ruled by small minorities unwilling to give up their privileges. If we are truly concerned with the role of the individual in society, we must transcend the exclusive concept of free elections and a multiparty system and look at the problem of democracy in *several dimensions*. I submit that the democratic character of a system can be judged only by looking at it from all aspects, of which the following four are the most important ones:

1). Political democracy in the Western sense: a multiparty system and free elections (provided they are real, and not sham).

2). An atmosphere of personal freedom. By this I mean a situation in which the individual can feel free to voice any opinion (including one critical of the government), without fear of any reprisals. It is clear that the degree of this personal freedom can vary. There can be, for instance, sanctions which pertain to a person's economic position but which do not threaten his personal freedom. There is a difference between the plain terror that existed under Stalin and the police atmosphere under Khrushchev. But though even the latter is greatly preferable to Stalin's terror, it does not constitute an atmosphere of personal freedom even in a restricted sense. However, according to all reports,

Poland and Yugoslavia, even though they are not democracies in terms of the first criterion, are societies in which personal freedom exists. This second aspect of democracy is so important because the possibility of living, thinking, speaking without fear of reprisal is of fundamental significance for the development of free men, even if they are not permitted to translate their views into political action.

3). An entirely different aspect of democracy is the economic one. If one wants to judge the role of the individual in any given country, one can not do so without examining for whose benefit the economic system works. If a system works mainly for the benefit of a small upper class, what is the use of free elections for the majority? Or rather, how can there be any authentically free election in a country which has such an economic system? Democracy is only possible in an economic system that works for the vast majority of the population. Here too, of course, are many variations. On the one extreme are systems where 90 per cent or more of the population do not share in the economic progress of the country (as is the case in many of the Latin American countries); on the other end are systems, like those of the United States and Great Britain, where, in spite of considerable inequality, there is a tendency toward increasing the equalization of economic benefits. What matters is that the democratic character of a country can not be judged without taking into account the fundamental economic situation.

4). Eventually there is a *social* criterion of democracy, namely the role of the individual in his work situation, and in the concrete decisions of his daily life. Does a system tend to turn people into conforming automatons, or does it tend to increase their individual activity and responsibility? Does it tend to centralize power and to decentralize power and decision-making, and thus secure democracy against the danger of dictators who by conquering the opposition *ipso facto* conquer the whole? Here again, there are many variations, and it is particularly important to examine not only the social role of the individual at a given moment, but the general trend within the system. Is it furthering or hindering individual development, responsibility, and decentralization?

If we are really concerned with democracy, we must be concerned with the chances a given system affords an individual to become a free, independent, and responsible participant in the life of his society. The full development of democracy depends on the presence of all four requirements mentioned above: political freedom, personal freedom, economic democracy, and social democracy. We can judge the democratic character of any country only if we take in account all four criteria, and then form an over-all judgment of the quality and the degree of democracy to be found in any given system. Our present method of paying attention only to the first criterion is unrealistic and will help only to defeat our world-wide propaganda for freedom and democracy.

If we apply these criteria concretely, we will find, for example, that the United States (and Great Britain) satisfy the criteria of political democracy, personal freedom (less than completely in the United States after the First World War and during the McCarthy period), and economic democracy. But, the active role of the individual is losing its importance with increasing bureaucratization. China, on the other hand, has neither political nor personal freedom, nor does it foster individual activity, but it has an economy geared to the welfare of the large majority. Yugoslavia does not have a multiparty system, but it has personal freedom, an economy which serves the majority, and it tends to encourage individual initiative and responsibility.

Returning to the "new world," it is clear that many countries do not have the necessary pre-conditions for a full-fledged democracy that satisfies all four of our criteria. Beyond that, the construction of a state-directed economy may make a full democracy impossible in a number of countries for quite some time. But provided criteria 2, 3, and 4 are present and developing, the absence of criterion 1—of free elections and a multiparty system—is not all that matters. If a society permits personal freedom, fosters economic justice, and encourages the expression of individual activity in economic and social life, I should think it can be called democratic, certainly with much more justification than states that are dominated economically by a minority, but that present a façade of political democracy. If we are truly concerned with the individual, we must stop thinking in clichés, and instead evaluate each country, including our own, from the standpoint of this multidimensional concept of democracy.

For a full-fledged democracy to be possible, several conditions are necessary. First of all, noncorrupt governments. A corrupt government morally undermines the whole citizenry from top to bottom, paralyzes initiative and hope, and makes planning and the use of outside economic aid more or less impossible.

In addition, planning is necessary primarily to use economic resources as adequately as possible. But it must also be added that planning and an honest government produce perhaps the most stimulating psychological reaction as far as the unfolding of human energy is concerned: *hope*. Hope and hopelessness are not primarily *individual* psychological factors; they are mainly created by the social situation of a country. If people have reasons to believe that they are marching toward a better future, they can move mountains. If they have no hope, they will stagnate and waste their energy.

Next to planning and an honest government, two other conditions are necessary: technical skill and capital. Here lies one of the great possibilities for the West (and for the Soviet Union) if they reconcile themselves to the support of democratic socialist regimes: they can give technical assistance and long-range cheap credits and grants to permit countries like India, Indonesia, etc., to develop an industry under much more favorable conditions than, for instance, China enjoyed. That country had very little economic aid from the outside compared, for instance, with the heavy capital investments that helped the industrialization of Czarist Russia.[49]

I have discussed in the foregoing remarks countries like India, which are already at the "take-off" stage. There are many other countries, like Iraq, which are still farther behind, economically speaking, and the newly created countries in Africa which are still in an

---

[49] Cf. for the whole problem W. W. Rostow, *The Stages of Economic Growth*, Harvard University Press, Cambridge, Mass., 1960, and the study by C. Kerr, J. Dunlop, F. Harbison, C. Myers, *Industrialism and Industrial Man*, Harvard University Press, Cambridge, Mass., 1960. The authors analyze the various forms of industrialization and at the same time of élites which guide it. Cf. also the paper by Henry G. Aubrey, Sino-Soviet Economic Activities in Less Developed Countries, publ. in *Congr. Committee Papers*, p. 45 ff., and Frank E. Trager, (ed.) *Marxism in Southeast Asia*, Stanford University Press, Stanford, 1960.

economically primitive stage. The methods for the economic development of these countries must be as varied as these countries are; nevertheless planning, government ownership of important sectors of the economy, honest government, foreign aid in acquiring technical skill and capital, will be necessary for these countries too.

One main objection to the suggestion to support democratic socialist systems in the underdeveloped countries will probably be that such systems will tend to join politically with the Russian–Chinese bloc, and be aligned against the West. This view sounds plausible only if one confuses Russian and Chinese communism with each other, and both with democratic socialism because they all have the words "Marxism" and "socialism" in common. But this is a fatal misunderstanding. Not only have democratic socialists all over the world shown their fundamental opposition to Russian or Chinese communism, not only have most of them always refused to enter even into alliances with the Communist "Marxists," but democratic socialism is, in fact, a much greater challenge to Russian and Chinese communism than any feudal or "capitalist" system in the underdeveloped countries. Such systems will eventually fall, but viable democratic socialist systems will demonstrate that the Russian–Chinese claim that their systems are the only alternative to capitalism is wrong. They will act as a dam to the political expansion of the Russian–Chinese bloc, but they can also serve as a bridge between that bloc and the United States–European bloc in a multicentered world.

The proposal I am making here is essentially in line with a statement by Professor Rostow: "It is therefore, as sure as anything can be that the central international problem for the future is the organization of a world community in which the United States, Western Europe, Japan, and Russia are joined by powerful industrial states in Asia, Latin America, the Middle East, and Africa—in about that order; and that, within something like seventy-five years, the bulk of the presently underdeveloped areas will have attained economic maturity."[50] The difference between us may lie in my emphasis that for many of the underdeveloped countries democratic-socialist systems will be necessary if the organization of an industrial world community is to be achieved.

The acceptance of this policy requires not only that we in the United States overcome deep-seated, yet erroneous clichés and irrational allergies toward certain words—such as socialism, government ownership of industries, etc. It requires, in addition, important changes in our dealings with our European allies and in our own policy in Latin America.

As far as our policy with regard to our European allies is concerned, we have already made a good beginning with Roosevelt's opposition to Churchill's wish to choose a war strategy that would help to preserve the British Empire. In President Eisenhower's post-Dulles period, he began to recognize African neutralism as legitimate, and the Kennedy administration has gone much further in this direction. We have accepted neutrality in Laos, have agreed to a United Nations resolution that demands Belgium's withdrawal from the Congo, have joined in the United Nations those powers that challenge the Portuguese dictatorial rule in Africa.

Yet, the real danger is that we will not go the whole way, and that we will permit our Western allies to push us into compromises with the last remnants of their

[50] W. W. Rostow, l.c. p. 413.

colonial policy, in exchange for their adherence to the Western alliance. We at first supported British pressure on Egypt, and only withdrew this support when the Suez attack brought us to the brink of war; we have not taken a clear stand in favor of Algerian independence, and it seems we have not been insistent enough to force the Belgians to relinquish their hold on the Congo. We shall be able to stop further Russian—but especially Chinese—successes in Asia and in Africa only if we have a clear and unequivocal policy of anti-colonialism.

The situation in Latin America is quite different. Here the United States is involved more directly. There are heavy United States investments in many Latin American countries, such as Venezuela, Argentina, Guatemala, and Cuba. The two latter countries are important examples of United States policy. In Guatemala the Arbenz government, which was not a "Communist government" although the Communists had a good deal of influence, was little interested in foreign policy. It was very much interested in domestic policy; it initiated labor laws that hurt the interests of the main economic power in Guatemala—the United Fruit Company.

A campaign began to accuse the Arbenz government of being Communist and, therefore, a threat to United States security. "Colonel Carlos Castillo Armas, an exile in Honduras, organized an expedition—with help which still remains mysterious[51]—to invade Guatemala. When the Guatemalan army virtually refused to fight Castillo Armas, Arbenz resigned and a few days later Castillo Armas became for all practical purposes

[51] To many observers the help was not as "mysterious" as the authors assume.

president of the republic. He organized an 'election' later in the year in which participants voted by show of hands, and he won by a 99 per cent majority.

"The Castillo Armas regime, in spite of the good intentions of the president, was a brutal dictatorship. Hundreds and perhaps thousands of peasants and workers were killed in a wave of revenge on the part of employers and landlords, who felt that they had been mistreated during the Arevalo-Arbenz period. The agrarian reform program started under Arbenz was reversed, and virtually all opposition was forbidden."[52]

The Guatemalan pattern opened a dangerous path for United States policy. Using the rationalization of fighting off a Communist threat, we helped destroy a legitimate government that was mainly preoccupied with measures to weaken the economic position and power of a great American corporation, the United Fruit Company. Is it surprising that many Latin Americans believe that we have found a new formula for the old "banana policy"? To them, our actions fit in the pattern that led to the occupation of the Philippines, Haiti, Cuba, Nicaragua, and the various aggressive acts against Mexico. Do they not have many reasons to believe that the big United States corporations prefer to deal with corrupt dictators like those who ruled Cuba, Venezuela, and Colombia than with popular and honest governments, and that many times United States official policy has been strongly influenced by these corporations?

At the time of writing, Cuba is our most acute problem in Latin America. We have occupied Cuba three times since the Spaniards left. We forced her into con-

[52] Charles O. Porter and Robert J. Alexander, *The Struggle for Democracy in Latin America*, The Macmillan Co., New York, 1961, p. 70.

ceding us a naval base we still use. The Platt Amendment, revoked only under Franklin D. Roosevelt, made Cuba legally a satellite. But despite the revocation, United States capital interests remained one of the most powerful political influences in Cuba. When popular protest eventually overthrew Batista, and Castro emerged as an admired national hero, there was little dissent. But Castro transformed the political revolution into a social and economic one. He has not only built houses, schools, and hospitals, he has nationalized the big sugar-growing estates, the oil industry, and banks, and thus has hurt the strong financial interests of those who had capital investments in Cuba.

"Of the *ten* big sugar companies that dominated the island's most important industry, *seven* were owned in the United States. Cuban participation in the United States sugar quota actually worked mostly to the advantage of these big producers, while the Cuban farm workers had for several years been living at or near the level of starvation. Many of Cuba's public utilities, banks, oil refineries, and extractive industries were also *owned by citizens of the United States.* Any social revolution would, therefore, necessarily adversely affect these property interests."[53]

As a result, a crescendo of hostility against Castro's government was unleashed, culminating in the accusation that he provided a foothold for Russian penetration of Latin America and a Communist base for an attack against the United States. In fact, the United States, after some initial hesitation, took a number of hostile actions against Cuba in the economic field: the cutting of the sugar quota, the embargo of almost all

[53] James P. Warburg, *Disarmament: The Challenge of the Nineteen Sixties,* Doubleday, New York, 1961, pp. 85–86.

trade, and the practical embargo on tourist trade, culminating in the break of diplomatic relations with
Cuba. At the same time an increasingly hostile mood
pervaded official and unofficial utterances on Cuba, until more recently anti-Castro rebels, morally and, it
seems, practically, supported by certain United States
groups, staged a counter-revolution.[54] All this was
done with the explanation that the Castro regime is
Russian-dominated, that Cuba is practically a Russian
satellite, and that the United States has a right and an
obligation to protect itself and the whole Western
Hemisphere from this Russian intrusion.

What are the facts? The Castro revolution was
an authentic Cuban revolution, and was in no way
helped or inspired by Moscow, Peiping, or the Cuban Communists who were allied with Batista during
most of his regime. The more the United States proceeded to threaten and strangle the Cuban economy,
the more was Castro forced to seek economic aid from
the Soviet bloc. As a consequence of his economic dependence on the Soviet bloc, Castro followed a pro-
Soviet line in his foreign policy, and the Cuban Communists, formerly held in contempt as the dishonest
opportunists they were and are, gained increasing influence. Statements about Castro's "communism" were
self-fulfilling predictions. Because of American measures, he was driven more and more into the Communist camp, and thus, retroactively, seemed to justify
the American policy.

As an additional proof of the accusations against

[54] At the time of revising this manuscript, an invasion
against the Castro regime has taken place, and has failed.
While it was not a direct intervention using United States
troops, it was, according to reports in *The New York Times*
and other sources, unofficially organized, financed, and supported by the United States.

Castro, American propaganda stresses the fact that so many former Castro adherents have now turned against him. However, it is obvious that, at first, almost one hundred per cent of the population were with Castro because everyone hated Batista. But when Castro transformed the political revolution into a social one (economically and socio-psychologically), it was natural that many members of the upper and middle classes were hurt, economically and socially, and went into opposition of Castro. It is even less surprising that they rationalized this opposition by claiming that Castro had become a tool of the Russians.

What about Communist policy in Cuba? First, Communists did not start the revolution. Second, Khrushchev was obliged to give assistance, if he wanted to retain his ideological role as the defender of the colonial world, and, even more important perhaps, if he wanted to counter the strong Chinese competition. He even declared that he would defend Cuba by nuclear retaliation if the United States intervened there militarily. Clearly, Khrushchev assumed that the United States would not intervene in such a manner, but none the less, he declared later that this offer of his had just been meant "symbolically," that is, he took it back.

The Russians bought Cuban sugar and granted credits, but only after heavy bargaining and by no means acceding to all the Cuban demands. In fact, it seems that Khrushchev has restrained Castro from being more aggressive. When Guevara came back from his visit to Moscow in the beginning of 1961 the Cuban government spoke of wanting a "new beginning" in Cuba–United States relations, and sent forth a number of "peace" feelers, which were all rejected by the United States.

Khrushchev's main aim is the ending of the cold war with the United States, and he knows that this would be impossible if he built a political, not to say military, base against the United States. There are good reasons for believing that Cuba would have joined the neutral camp, had the United States not insisted that she must remain in our sphere of interest and exercised heavy economic pressure on her.

The fundamental question is this: What is the real motivation behind United States policy toward Castro? There are several possibilities: 1) That we will not permit the existence of a social revolution (that goes beyond pious words) anywhere in Latin America, because such a revolution threatens American financial interests not only in the country concerned but, by its example, in all Latin America. 2) That we will not permit the existence of a regime that is not based on free elections and that restricts freedom of the press and of speech. 3) That we will not tolerate the existence of a country in Latin America that follows in its foreign policy—and to some extent ideologically—a pro-Russian line. 4) That we will not tolerate the existence of a regime that is the result of a Russian military conquest (such as Poland or Hungary).

It hardly needs to be said that it is not our policy to attempt the overthrow of undemocratic regimes in the Western Hemisphere. It is also clear that in Europe we do support socialist regimes, like Poland and Yugoslavia, provided they take a neutral position (as Yugoslavia does), or even only a somewhat independent position (as Poland does). Is it different in Latin America, when important United States financial interests are involved? Although the Castro revolution was not the result of a Russian-organized coup, and Cuba is by no means a Russian satellite, it is true that the Castro government by now is politically allied with the Russian bloc, and that the Cuban Communists seem to be increasingly influential in the government. To the extent to which this is the case, I, like anyone else who does not desire the spread of Russian or Chinese communism, regret this. But I believe that the only thing that transforms the Communist influence in Cuba into a threat against the United States and the Western Hemisphere is precisely the policy of the United States. If we had accepted Cuba as a neutral—which she would probably prefer to be—or even as a Russian international fellow traveler, and if in spite of this we had assisted Cuba economically, rather than tried to strangle her, Cuba would pose no threat against anyone. Even if Castro-type revolutions were to occur in other Latin American countries, they would be no threat to the existence of the United States. But if we insist that whoever is not for us is against us and if we give aid to anyone who wants to regain his lost properties, we shall in the long run earn for ourselves only the hatred of all Latin American peoples and especially of the rising new generation of leaders.

The assumption that Russia needs a military base against the United States is a thought which would have been perfectly reasonable even ten years ago, but which is unreal now at a time when Russian rockets can reach us in less than thirty minutes—and a submarine practically instantly.[55]

I suggest that we must face the facts squarely. Even the most developed Latin American countries have a per-capita living standard that is less than one-tenth that of the United States. The relative growth rates of these Latin American countries are lagging behind the United States, and the gap between the two worlds

[55] It is too little known in the United States that there are a great number of anti-Communist, democratic socialists in many Latin American countries who are fervently on the side of Castro's revolution. The recently elected Senator Palacios from Buenos Aires is an excellent example.

is widening rather than narrowing. Fundamental measures of planning, state interpolation, etc., will be necessary in all Latin America. If the government of the United States supports the selfish interests of American corporations by its policies in Latin America, it may keep some of the existing systems in power. But, we shall convince the broad masses, especially the politically effective younger generation of middle-class intellectuals, that the Communists are right in their accusation that fundamental economic changes that hurt American capital will be prevented by the United States. They will then accept the fact that only an anti-American Communist revolution can guarantee the necessary economic reforms.

In Latin America we are conducting a short-term policy that in the long run will lead to catastrophe. A policy that puts the long-term interest of the United States above particular corporate interests will permit a peaceful, yet fundamental, social-economic evolution of Latin America with our assistance. This means withholding political support from big corporations, which wield a power in many Latin American countries that United States law denies them within the borders of the United States.

IV) CONCLUSIONS

The situation in which humanity finds itself is exceedingly grave. The policy of the deterrent will not ensure peace; it will most likely destroy civilization, and it will certainly destroy democracy even if it preserves peace. The first steps in avoiding a nuclear cataclysm and preserving democracy are to agree on universal disarmament, and, simultaneously, to arrive at a *modus vivendi* with the Soviet Union based on the acceptance of existing possessions of the two blocs.

Suggestions for peace

These steps, however, are only a beginning in coping with the immediate danger of nuclear war. They do not solve the world problem in the long run. The central issue today is that of the future course of the underdeveloped nations, which comprise the majority of the human race. They insist not only on obtaining political independence but also on rapid economic development. They will not wait two hundred years to achieve the economic level of Europe or the United States. The Communists have shown that by means of force and fanaticism it is possible to attain results; their method will become irresistibly attractive unless it can be demonstrated that similar results can be achieved without terror and without the destruction of individuality, through central planning along with economic and technical assistance from the industrialized countries. Such a policy requires the acceptance of a neutral bloc by both the East and the West and the strengthening of the United Nations as a supernational organization charged with the administration of disarmament and economic aid.

The pursuit of the policy suggested here requires such drastic changes in the American attitude that one cannot avoid having serious doubts whether such a policy is possible; in fact, its acceptance would seem to be impossible unless there is a growing conviction that it constitutes the only alternative to war.

First, such a policy would require that the President and Congress subordinate the special interests of the armed forces and of the big corporations (especially those with strong capital investments abroad) to the main goals of United States policy, peace and survival as a democratic nation.

Furthermore, this policy requires a material and spiritual reorientation in the West entailing the replacement of projective-paranoid attitudes toward communism by an objective and realistic appraisal of the facts. Such realism is only possible if we take a critical view of ourselves and recognize the discrepancy that exists between our professed ideals and our actions. We claim that our present system is characterized by a high degree of individualism, and of religious or secular humanism. In reality we are a managerial, industrial society with a diminishing amount of individualism. We like to produce more and to consume more, but we have no goal—either as individuals or as a nation. We are developing into faceless organization men, alienated from ourselves and lacking authentic feelings and convictions. This very fact leads us to put so much emphasis on the lack of freedom and individualism in Russia because we can then protest against features of the Soviet society which in reality we are approaching in our own.

The Russians are today in some respects where Americans were one hundred years ago; they are building a society, full of hope and enthusiasm to go ahead and to accomplish what they have set out to do. While in the United States, although there is still unnecessary poverty and unnecessary suffering, we are only filling out what has been left to do; we are only doing more of the same. We have no vision of something new, no aim that truly inspires us. If this continues, we and the West will not survive. We will lack the energy and vitality that are necessary for any nation or group of nations to live and to survive in a world that is witnessing the awakening of nations that have been silent for hundreds of years. Our weapons will not save us—at best they will drag our enemies into the holocaust thirty minutes after we have perished.

What can save us and what can help mankind is a renaissance of the spirit of humanism, of individualism, and of America's anti-colonialist tradition. By our hesitant and often ambiguous policy toward the underdeveloped peoples we have helped the Communists realize one of their most significant successes: to become the leaders in the historical movement of the "New World," and to stamp us as the "reactionary" forces trying to arrest the historical trend. We must, if not surpass, at least equal the Communists, by being wholly and unreservedly with the wave of history, rather than halfheartedly and hesitatingly. As has been said over and over again, the present struggle is a struggle for men's minds. One can not win this struggle with empty slogans and propaganda tricks, which nobody except their own authors believe. One can win it only if one has ideas to offer that are authentic because they are rooted in the realities of a nation's life.

The West is old, but by no means exhausted. It has shown its vitality by achievements in scientific thought that are unparalleled in history. We are suffering not so much from exhaustion as from the absence of goals, and from the "doublethink" that paralyzes us. If we ask ourselves where we are and where we are going, we shall have a chance to formulate new goals socially, economically, politically, and spiritually.

The Soviet system challenges us to develop a system that can satisfy the needs of man better than communism does. But while we talk a great deal about freedom and the superiority of our system, we avoid the Soviet challenge and prefer to describe communism as an international conspiracy out to conquer the world by force and subversion. The Russians hope to see the victory of communism as the result of its superior performance. Are we afraid that we can not meet the Communist competition, and is this the reason why we prefer to define the struggle as a military one rather than as a socio-economic one? Are we unwilling to make the necessary changes within our own society, and do we, for this reason, declare that no essential changes are necessary? Are we afraid to curb the political influence of our corporate investors in Latin America? By concentrating on the military threat against us and the resulting arms race we miss the *one* chance for victory: to demonstrate that it is possible to have at home—and in Asia, Africa, and Latin America—economic progress *and* individuality, economic and social planning *and* democracy. This is the answer to the Communist challenge—not the nuclear deterrent.

Our present thinking is a symptom of a deep-seated, though unconscious defeatism, of a lack of faith in the very values which we proclaim. We only cover up this defeatism by concentrating on the evils of communism and by promoting hate. If we continue with our policy of the deterrent and with our unholy alliances with dictatorial states in the name of freedom, we shall defeat the very values we hope to defend. We shall lose our freedom and probably also our lives.

What matters today is preserving the world; but in order to preserve it, certain changes have to be made, and in order to make these changes, historical trends have to be understood and anticipated.

All men of good will or, rather, all men who love life must form a united front for survival, for the continuation of life and civilization. With all the scientific and technical progress man has made, he is bound to solve the problem of hunger and poverty, and he can afford to try solutions in different directions. There is only one thing he can *not* afford—and that is to go on with preparations for war, which, this time, will lead to catastrophe. There is still time to anticipate the next historical development and to change our course. But unless we act soon we shall lose the initiative, and circumstances, institutions, and weapons, which we created, will take over and decide our fate.

ANCHOR BOOKS

DOLPHIN BOOKS AND DOLPHIN MASTERS

The bold face M indicates a Dolphin Master. Dolphin Masters are Dolphin Books in the editions of greatest importance to the teacher and student. In selecting the Dolphin Masters, the editors have taken particular pains to choose copies of the most significant edition (usually the first) by obtaining original books or their facsimiles or by having reproductions made of library copies of particularly rare editions. Facsimiles of original title pages and other appropriate material from the first edition are included in many Masters.

FICTION